How to Grow Old Disgracefully

ALSO BY HERMIONE GINGOLD

Sirens Should Be Seen and Not Heard

The World is Square

HERMIONE GINGOLD

How to Grow Old Disgracefully

TIDIED UP BY HER FRIEND
ANNE CLEMENTS EYRE

LONDON
VICTOR GOLLANCZ LTD
1989

First published in the USA 1988 by
St Martin's Press, New York

First published in Great Britain 1989
by Victor Gollancz Ltd,
14 Henrietta Street, London WC2E 8QJ

British Library Cataloguing in Publication Data
Gingold, Hermione
    How to grow old disgracefully
    1. Theatre. Acting. Gingold, Hermione
    I. Title   II. Eyre, Anne Clements
    792'.028'0924

    ISBN 0-575-04477-2

ACKNOWLEDGEMENTS

With grateful thanks to Mrs Kathleen Tynan and Mr Anton
Troxler of Paradise Films, Samuel French Ltd, Mr Angus
McBean and the Harvard Theatre Collection, Mr Sheridan
Morley, *The Times*, the *Daily Telegraph*, the *Birmingham
Post and Mail*, Mr Ronnie Cass, Miss Zoe Dominic, Miss
Martha Swope, Phototeque, M.G.M. archives, The Mander
and Micheson Theatre Collection, Mr Sid Colin, L. Arnold
Weissberger and Mr Leonard Strauss.

Every effort has been made to trace copyright ownership of
the photographs, lyrics and extracts used in this book.

Photoset in Great Britain by
Rowland Phototypesetting Ltd, Bury St Edmunds, Suffolk
and printed by St Edmundsbury Press Ltd
Bury St Edmunds, Suffolk

*I dedicate this book to all my dear friends
without whose help it would have been written
in half the time.*

Contents

List of Photographs

PROLOGUE
by Lady Eyre

The death of Hermione Ferdinanda Gingold on May 24th, 1987, made the front page in newspapers on both sides of the Atlantic.

She completed this autobiography shortly before she died.

Hermione was known as the last of the great British eccentrics, once dubbed "the funniest woman in the world". Audiences loved her devastating wit and revelled in her reputation as man-eater, witch, and monstrous queen of high camp.

She claimed, "I never try to be funny, dear, it's just that I have a certain slant on life."

The late W. A. Darlington of the *Daily Telegraph* said, "For those who never had the experience of watching her at work, she must remain beyond imagination." Kenneth Tynan attempted to analyse her special magic with the words, "She can turn a melting smile into a baring of fangs more outrageously than anyone I know except Groucho Marx, and she gets her laughs by this method of suddenly and fleetingly letting us glimpse the caged wolf pacing up and down behind the facade of the Grande Dame. If we must define what she does, we can only call it self-mockery." While Sheridan Morley wrote in *The Times*, "Miss Hermione Gingold is an original: a 100 per cent solid gold eccentric. She's also her own invention and contribution to the twentieth century. The proud possessor of a face that has clearly launched a thousand jokes and a voice that makes Edith Evans's Lady Bracknell sound positively suburban."

As an actress, her career spanned seventy-eight vigorous years:

11

from childhood appearances on the British stage with a young Noël Coward; in Shakespeare at London's Old Vic Theatre; in her outrageous comedy performances in West End and Broadway revues; and in her enduring film roles in *The Music Man*, *A Little Night Music*, and *Gigi*, in which her unforgettable bittersweet duet with Maurice Chevalier— "Ah yes, I remember it well"—has become a screen classic. Aged eighty-one, she was again the toast of Broadway in *Side by Side by Sondheim*. The same year, she embarked on her last great love affair—with a young man fifty-five years her junior—complaining, "The trouble with men is that there aren't enough of them."

Her classic brand of throwaway sarcasm made her a popular television chat-show guest. When Jack Paar referred to an actress called Zsa Zsa, Hermione asked, "Zsa Zsa who?" She dismissed Elsa Maxwell as being "just another pretty face", and when she was asked, "Hermione, is your husband still living?" she drawled, "It's a matter of opinion."

She didn't suffer fools gladly and could crush lesser chat-show hosts with a withering glance and a quip from her basso profundo voice, once described as "powdered glass in deep syrup".

A young playwright asking her opinion of his script was told, "My dear boy, in future I advise you never to write anything more ambitious than a grocery list."

The paradox of Gingold was that her friends knew a gentler, warmer side to her—a woman of vulnerability, unswerving in her loyalty, devoted to animals, and constantly funny and exciting to be with. In fact, most of them agreed an hour away from Hermione was like a month in the country.

Even a casual shopping trip with her was outrageous fun. "I think I'll buy these pink shoes—they'll draw attention away from my face." Although always polite and gracious, she'd say in an aside, "Don't ask that assistant—she's obviously a half-wit"; and she could query, "Will it wash?" with enough force to reduce a shop girl to a trembling jelly.

A young man came up to her, saying he was engaged in public relations, and her quip, "Oh I prefer to keep my relations private," stopped him in his tracks. Inevitably, fans would cluster and she was usually very courteous to them; but once in a Manhattan restaurant, I noticed a man staring at her. He eventually plucked up enough courage to come over and enquire, "It is Hermione Gingold, isn't it?" She fixed him with an icy glare. "Who?" she boomed. His courage was failing rapidly but he stuttered, "Er, I thought—you look like Hermione Gingold." "I've never heard of her," she said dismissively, and with an almost imperceptible twinkle, added, "She must be very ugly."

As we continued our lunch, she sighed and said, "When I was your age, I swore I'd kill myself if I ever lived to be forty; when I was forty, I swore I'd kill myself when I became fifty; now I'm over sixty and I'd love some more of those dee-licious raspberries."

When Hermione last came to stay with me in London, she arrived, claiming, "I'm suffering from jet lag." (She'd come by ship.) Although she was over eighty, in her luggage she carried a skipping rope. She'd been told skipping would be good therapy for her injured arm. Not only was she full of plans for a new Broadway revue to be called *Déjà Revu* but she was talking about travelling to Egypt to do a trip up the Nile in a few years' time. Every day her dynamism showed she had no realistic idea of her age.

Hermione often threatened to write her memoirs when she retired. Friends and lovers, not to mention ex-husbands, began quaking in their shoes when she promised to name names and tell all. As she passed eighty and showed no signs whatever of retiring, they breathed sighs of relief and felt they were in the clear. While on tour in *Side by Side by Sondheim*, she had an accident that forced a temporary retirement and at last her threat became a reality.

"Darling," she said, her voice swooping through two octaves, "after one's dead, people write such terrible things about one. Of course in my case they'll all be true, but I'd rather write them myself and get the record straight."

The Gingold residence went strangely quiet, but for one who so loved life, the lure of entertainments and company was hard to eschew and the self-imposed purdah required of an author was difficult for a hedonist of Miss G's calibre to maintain. Despite a large advance from her publisher, enquiries on how the tome was progressing were received with an unusual reticence.

One day my phone rang. "Anney Panney," she pleaded across the Atlantic, "will you help me with the book? I wanted Norman Mailer or Gore Vidal and although I've offered them the outrageous sum of fifty dollars, they've both turned me down."

Willingly, I promised to lock her in her room, throw away the key, and for each written page she slipped under the door, I promised to slip back a flattened chocolate macaroon. (You could get Gingold to do almost anything for a chocolate macaroon.)

La Gingold knew exactly what she wanted to say and how she wanted to say it. She'd learned much from her two writer husbands and had written much of her own comedy material as well as two spoof fantasy autobiographies. She required no assistance from me, merely bribes to stick at it.

Tentatively, I proffered a few memory-jogging ideas. "You'll have to mention Hermione Baddeley," I said bravely. "Take those words out of your mouth—you don't know where they've been," she retorted. I tried again. "What about that lovely story of your mother telling you the facts of life, when all she said was 'never sit on a strange lavatory seat,' and then retired to bed for three days?"

She smiled nostalgically, then grimaced and delivered the verbal whiplash, "I don't care to reduce my book to that lavatorial level." In stony silence, she disappeared to her room and slipped the anecdote into her book the following day.

My task was chiefly confined to deciphering her totally illegible longhand, adding some punctuation, and keeping an eye open for the more obvious libel suits. As each page emerged, it became clear that what she was producing was not only a fascinating record of a life sacrificed to art and pleasure but an extremely funny book written in her own inimitable style.

One day, in a mood of uncharacteristic self-effacement, she

14

suddenly said she wanted the book to say "by Hermione Gingold" in large letters and "tidied up by Anne Clements Eyre" in smaller letters underneath. I was genuinely touched.

Sadly, Hermione died shortly after she completed the final draft of her book. In accordance with her wishes in wanting to "get the record straight", it has been decided to publish it posthumously.

It would have been such a loss to deprive readers of a truly funny book, written by a remarkable lady. For Hermione Gingold was unique and her like will never pass this way again.

Anne Clements Eyre
London, January, 1989

1
ENGLAND:

*"Land of Hope and Glory,
Mother of the Free"*

There's nothing so ageing as the past—especially when it catches up with you. I like to live in the present but I'm going to make a great effort to delve deep into my past and tell it as it was and is, and to hell with scruples.

Writing one's memoirs is a difficult task. What should one leave out and what would be of interest? How much is one willing to expose to the raised eyebrow? My reputation's pretty bad already and I have been reluctant to make it worse, but I've decided it will be wonderful to get the whole nasty mess off my chest.

The story of my life is so strange that it has me wondering how I ever lived through it and stayed sane.

I was born on December 9th, 1897, and Queen Victoria was sitting on the throne, although she was so old, I think she had to be carried on and off.

I don't know exactly where I was born but it was somewhere in London, and my first years were spent in a large house in Maida Vale, which in those days was quite a chic neighbourhood. My father, James Gingold, was a stockbroker and my mother also had a lot of time on her hands.

My paternal grandfather was Viennese and his wife was Turkish. She came from a large family of Turkish opera singers. Apparently, her family was very possessive and to get her away from their clutches, my grandfather took her to London, where they settled and became naturalised English.

My father had four brothers and one sister. The brothers I

hardly remember at all, and his sister—I'll come to her later. Sooner than that, in fact.

The five brothers were all very tall. Their sister Helene was six feet tall and was known to us as Aunt Baby. Aunt Baby was a baroness. I'm not certain how she came by this title but I think it had something sexy to do with the king of Greece.

She also claimed she was colonel of a Greek regiment. Sometimes she'd hire a box at the theatre and take my sister and me to matinées. When people stared in amazement at this six-foot apparition wearing a sky blue uniform and a tall hat with plumes, she'd say, "Anyone would think they'd never seen a woman in uniform before," which was probably quite true at that time. If you went to the theatre with her at night, she wore a Greek toga with grapes in her hair, and people not only stared but were heard to say, "She must be advertising something."

She wrote poems and books, one of which is dedicated to "My Uncle Nicola Nisco St Giorgio Mantagna, Senator and Historian Royal of Italy", which I think sounds grand but slightly phoney. I like to think that all this Turkish-Italian-Austrian blood rushing through my veins gives me a perfect excuse for my rather un-English behaviour.

I believe I may also have some Roumanian blood, a legacy from a grandmother on my father's side who was a great traveller.

My parents were complete opposites. My father was wildly extravagant; he possessed forty pairs of handmade shoes, twenty sets of monogrammed silk pyjamas, and eight Louis Vuitton trunks. In his lifetime, he went through three fortunes, only one of which he made himself.

He was handsome, amusing, and completely unscrupulous. I'm still puzzled as to why he married my mother, whose maiden name was Kate Walter. She came from a well-to-do Jewish family and was one of ten sisters who were great beauties, except three. My mother was one of the three.

Considering my aunts all had a strict upbringing and were brought up to be ladies, their endings were diverse.

Mother and the Aunts—or Mother's Sisters

GLADYS: Died young; never met her.

PHYLLIS: Very pretty; was kept, though not entirely, by a millionaire. She also had a young man on the side.

JUDY: Had a lover called Toddles who was married and wouldn't get a divorce, so she pined away. By the way, it took a long time.

DOLLY: Acted as secretary to her rich brother. Had an affair with a nice little Jewish man, then married him and lived happily until he died.

VIOLET: Married; had two children. Died suddenly, of what, the doctors didn't know.

NELLIE: Very bad temper; smart but plain; never married. Owned an expensive millinery business just off Bond Street with Gertie.

GERTIE: Very pretty and sang beautifully. She married her lover at the age of forty-three and then had a baby called Patricia, who when she grew up had an affair with my second husband.

BETTY: My favourite. She was funny and cosy. Although she wasn't pretty, she married twice and had a huge house off Baker Street with numerous bedrooms, which she always kept filled.

HANNAH: Plain, very nice, and the only sensible one of the family. She was at one time matron of a London hospital and later had her own nursing home.

KATE: Was my mother and also my sister Margaret's.

ARTHUR: Was the rich one of the family. He married Doris Joel; they had a son who died, and the marriage broke up. Any member of the family needing money went to him and was never refused.

STANLEY: Very short. Married Hannah Dee. They had a daughter named Olive. She was a very bad child but calmed down as she grew up and played the lead in *The Blue Bird* at the Haymarket Theatre. She would have been a wonderful ballet dancer but she got too fat. She became a lesbian, married a gay boy, went to Australia, and was never heard of again.

As you can see, I came from pretty bad stock, and if you want to grow old disgracefully—it helps!

My mother wasn't at all like her sisters. She was very proper and extremely boring. Once, to liven things up, my father suggested inviting a neighbour round for tea and light conversation. My mother refused, saying, "I will not have that woman in the house. She dyes her hair."

That was the sort of woman my mother was. She disapproved of almost everyone. Her sister Dolly used to write poetry, and my mother used to refer to her with great disdain as "your Aunt Bohemia". My mother was also a hypochondriac and her ambition in life was to become a chronic invalid. You could write the feelings of love I have for my mother on the head of a pin and still have room for the Lord's Prayer.

Would anyone in their right mind inflict the name Hermione Ferdinanda Gingold on a babe in arms? That was the name my mother chose for me. My younger sister was simply called Margaret.

Perhaps the silliest question I've ever been asked is whether Hermione Ferdinanda Gingold was my real name. As if anyone would *choose* a name like that—except my mother. I think the

Ferdinanda was in memory of my Uncle Ferdinand, and Hermione from Shakespeare's *The Winter's Tale*, which she was reading just before my birth. I suppose I should be grateful it wasn't *Hamlet* or I might have been Ham. Actually, I'm now quite glad my name is Hermione Gingold because it's such a long name that on theatre billboards there isn't room for another name beside it.

My mother told me people used to look at me in my pram and exclaim, "What a very ugly baby!" Strangely enough, I grew into a very beautiful golden-haired child, only to revert to complete ugliness again when I grew up—though I've always been attractive, especially to men.

My sister and I lived at the top of the house in our own little world, shut off from life by a gate at the top of the stairs. In charge of us were a nurse and an undernurse whose main function was to protect our parents from our unsolicited visits. If we wanted to see our parents, we had to make an appointment. We saw our mother at teatime; our father hardly at all.

Occasionally, though, as a treat, he would take my sister and me to the Savoy for tea. Sometimes a very beautiful redheaded woman took tea with us, and with hindsight I wonder whether she was his mistress.

When I was quite small, my wealthy grandfather left my sister and me quite a sum of money, but we never received a penny of it. My father had been made trustee of our inheritance and he spent the lot. I didn't mind; he was such fun, I'd have given him anything.

I was taken by my nurse to see Queen Victoria's funeral. Through the mists of memory, I think I can hear the sombre music played by the bands and see the black plumes on the horses' heads, but I also have a recollection of huge crowds cheering and waving; and as I'm quite sure there were no jubilant crowds at Queen Victoria's funeral, I may be confusing it with Edward the Seventh's coronation, to which I was also taken.

We two girls lived in our little world quite pleasantly. In fact, we lived so normally I shall skip on to our first move.

There was suddenly a great change in our lifestyle. I don't know why we left Maida Vale but I have an idea it was because my father had lost a lot of money on the stock exchange. My father was always very rich or very poor; there was never any in-between. When he was rich, he showered my sister and me with extravagant presents and when he was poor, he used to break into my piggy bank. It seemed we were now very poor. We kept Nurse Morgan but it was goodbye to the undernurse and the day nursery and the night nursery, and we went to live with my aunt and my grandmother who lived not far from Maida Vale.

I don't remember much about life in Boundary Road. My Turkish grandmother used to scandalise St John's Wood by sitting cross-legged on the floor smoking a hookah; my aunts quarrelled; and my mother tried hard to become a semi-invalid. There was a large garden at the back of the house in which I spent a lot of my time with my spade, digging, in the hope of getting down under to Australia, where I understood from my father people walked upside down.

In the garden, there was also a disused potting shed. A home and homemaking have always been very important to me. Maybe it was because we'd just lost our own home, but I started making a home in the potting shed. After getting rid of all the pots, I painted the shed myself and decorated it with paper lanterns and cutouts from magazines. When I'd finished, it looked so pretty I asked my mother's permission to move in permanently. She refused.

After a little time in Boundary Road, my father disappeared, to reappear for our next move to a small attic flat in Cricklewood, which was, and still is, a rather depressing suburb. Here I was sent to Miss Gomm's kindergarten. I must admit I was a terrible pupil and cheated wherever possible. I'm sure the only reason I was allowed to stay on was because of my appearance in the end-of-term school plays. Even Miss Gomm herself said my Cardinal Wolsey was memorable. I managed to finish my final speech in spite of the fact that my cotton-wool beard had stuck in my throat and I could hardly breathe. It is only with hindsight that I realised what a strange choice Shakespeare's *Henry VIII* was for a kinder-garten play. Of course, I didn't understand a word I was saying but I gave it all I'd got, which even in those days was quite a lot. It was then I decided if ever I grew up, I would be an actress.

My next part was Sleeping Beauty. I was rather taken with the little boy who was playing the part of the Prince. He had to kiss me awake, and I told him we should practise the scene on our own. Fishing for a compliment, I said coyly, "I can't think why I was chosen. I'm not nearly beautiful enough." "You could wear a mask," he said.

I thoroughly enjoyed kindergarten, but my mother decided to have me educated at home, as she thought schools were a hotbed of measles, mumps, etcetera, and so I left Miss Gomm's. On the whole, I think they were rather pleased to see me go.

At home I had more time for mischief. I poked the eyes out of my sister's dolls and I teased her unmercifully. I suffered from curvature of the spine and its miserable treatment entailed lying flat on the floor with weights placed upon my stomach for several hours a day. I didn't take this treatment lying down.

I really was a horrid child and also a strange one. I used to walk in my sleep and when I wasn't walking at night, I had a go at trying to visualise eternity and space. This led me to have the most awful nightmares night after night.

Although we weren't brought up to be any particular religion, we were taught to say our prayers. I remember one that ended, "Thy glorious kingdom, which is for ever and ever. Amen." These words made me scream, "I don't want to be anywhere for ever and ever. It's too much." To me, anything—even a gracious kingdom—that went on forever seemed to be the most frighten-ing thing in the world. My parents tried to soothe me and they managed to, temporarily. Funnily enough, eternity still worries me, but now no one arrives to soothe me.

Rich or poor, we always went *en famille* to the seaside for our summer holidays. One year we went to Cornwall, where my father built a great kite. It really was huge, even taller than he was. He told me he was going to try to fly up into space on it. Of course it was so heavy it never even got off the ground; but it shows you how desperate he was to get away from my mother.

It was on this holiday that I insisted on being photographed in my bathing dress. You can see this picture facing page 32 and I think it is quite charming. However, my mother was very upset at me being photographed in a bathing dress. She was afraid the picture would be sent to Paris by devious means and be placed for sale among filthy pictures where it would be bought by a British tourist who would tell a friend of the family. She was so upset that she refused to eat meat for five days and hardly spoke to me till I reached the age of seventeen.

The first sign that men were going to be important in my life came when my mother asked me whom I'd like to invite to my sixth birthday party. I said, without the slightest hesitation, "The butcher's boy." He was my hero and delivered the meat on a kind of stretcher that he carried on his broad shoulders. My mother went into apoplexy at my unexpected choice and said firmly, "No."

Cherry pie was my favourite dessert. Tinker, tailor, soldier, sailor . . . I used to count my cherry stones with more concentration than my governess thought proper and she complained to my mother, "Hermione is perhaps a little advanced for her age."

Our family fortunes must have improved, for our next move was to a flat in York Street, off Baker Street.

I enjoyed living at York Street enormously. It was a madhouse full of interesting people. The landlady of the house had been a great beauty and was still very striking to look at. She had two lovely children and two who were not so bad. Her daughter Flora was a beautiful girl, and her son Reggie Sheffield eventually went to Hollywood to play Tarzan's son. His mother knew Marconi who invented the wireless. Marconi used to visit the house and he brought Reggie a radio; it was one of the first in the country.

I loved Flora, and sometimes when one of my aunts came to stay, I was sent to sleep with her. I said "sleep", but mostly I stayed awake watching her and wondering what she'd do if I touched her. But I never dared to.

So far my acting experience had been confined to kindergarten, but at York Street I was forever organising the Sheffield children and my sister and cousins into little plays and concert parties that we'd put on to entertain the other occupants of the house and my admiring aunts. Naturally, I saw to it that I was always the leading lady.

For our next family holiday, we went to Broadstairs, and it was there that I made my first public appearance. I was about six years old and on the beach I came upon Uncle Mac's Minstrel Show. I was enchanted by it, and the songs they sang I can remember to this day.

> *The other night I did call on Miss Brown.*
> *She was having her bath so she could not come down.*
> *I said, "Slip on something, come down for a tick."*
> *So she slipped on the soap and she did come down quick.*

> *There was an old woman of Cheadle*
> *Who when in church sat on a needle.*
> *The needle was threaded so was not embedded*
> *And was easily pulled out by the beadle.*

After the first half of their show, they invited children in the audience to come up on to their platform, and I raced up to sing a song. "God Save the King" was the only song I could think of at short notice. When I finished, I burst into tears and howled my head off until they gave me first prize. The applause went to my head like champagne.

From that moment on, I devoted all my energies to begging my

27

parents to allow me to go on the stage. At first, my mother was appalled, but when we returned to London, she did something rather sensible for once. She decided that if I was insistent on going into the theatre, I'd better study properly for it. With great joy, I began to have singing, piano, and fencing lessons, dancing lessons with Madame Carmani, and acting lessons with the great Rosina Filippi. She was a wonderful teacher, wise and kindly yet awe-inspiring. They were happy days for me.

Our next move was to the other, cheaper end of York Street. My father and sister didn't come to join us. Where they went and why, I haven't a clue. They eventually returned looking very suntanned and my father declared he had decided to become a Buddhist.

Later in life, I asked my father why he had embraced Buddhism and he said it was because the Buddhists were kind to animals and didn't squash spiders. Neither he nor my mother ever tried to influence my sister or me to become Buddhist, Jewish, Christian, Seventh-Day Adventist, or anything else because they said we should keep an open mind and choose our own religion when we grew up and knew more about life. I suppose I'm as grown-up now as I ever will be and rapidly approaching my second childhood before I'm even through my first. The more I see of life, the less I feel I know about it, so I'm still trying to make up my mind which religion I should choose. You could say I'm open to offers.

It was in the second York Street flat that I fell in love for the first time. He was a medical student who lived on the first floor. I used to sit on the stairs waiting for him to come home. He took absolutely no notice of me, and later on when I had bronchial pneumonia, I kept calling for him. My mother was very embarrassed but she went and asked him to come and see me. He did and as I got better, I forgot all about him, but my mother was beginning to realise she had a problem on her hands.

28

I was ten years old when Miss Filippi sent me to audition for Sir Herbert Beerbohm Tree at His Majesty's Theatre. I was auditioning for a part in *Pinkie and the Fairies*. Fairies had quite a different connotation in those days. I had been told I would be required to sing and I elected to trill "Two Eyes of Grey", a silly grown-up song.

Two eyes of grey
That used to be so
  bright.
Where is the shadow
Veiling all that light.
Why do the tears
Usurp the place
Of just the sweetest light
I saw in any woman's
  face.
It breaks my heart,
To see those two grey
  eyes
So sad . . .

After I'd sung it, I remember Beerbohm Tree patting me on the head and saying, "It's not a very suitable song for a child." But I got the part of the Herald.

My first part, and if only I could have realised how lucky I was—what a company! Ellen Terry and Lady Tree as the two aunts; Marie Löhr played Cinderella, Viola Tree was the Sleeping Beauty, and Mrs Patrick Campbell's daughter Stella played Mollie.

The great Ellen Terry was by that time an old lady and nearly blind. When she first saw my stage makeup, she said, "You have terrible makeup, dear." I thought, She's so blind—how can she tell? She took me to my dressing room and redid my makeup. As she peered through her glasses, her nose to my nose, I remember

29

hoping she wouldn't poke my eye out by mistake. I didn't have any idea what a great honour she was doing me.

It was a wonderful first engagement. Each day all the children were given a tea of a soft-boiled egg and bread and butter under the dome at the top of the theatre.

As the Herald, I wore a beautiful costume. Red tights, a tabard, and I had a long gold trumpet that I had to manoeuvre around the stage. W. Graham Robertson, who wrote the play, sent me some red roses and asked whether he could paint a portrait of me wearing my Herald's costume. I wrote back a thank you letter, starting "Dear Sir". When I told my mother, she was horrified.

"Only tradespeople write letters starting 'Dear Sir'," and she practically fainted at the idea of me becoming an artist's model, so that was the end of that.

Beerbohm Tree made me understudy to Pinkie and wrote in my autograph album: "Just an understudy to start with but such a good one." Ellen Terry wrote: "Sweet Hermione Gingold, on we go and my love goes with you."

My autograph book was my most-treasured possession and, like a fool, I burnt it many years later. It was when my first husband, Michael Joseph, was dangerously ill; his hospital nurse said I should burn my most-treasured possession as a sacrifice to God and then pray for his recovery. So I did just that. It worked. Then I left him.

In Beerbohm Tree's company was the actor Henry Ainley. I fell madly in love with him and followed him about like a shadow, hoping one day he would notice me, and sure enough he did. As a matter of fact, he practically fell over me. "They are turning this theatre into a crêche," he murmured as he disentangled my curls from his shoelaces. I was completely crushed and brokenhearted for at least ten days.

When *Pinkie and the Fairies* finished its London season, the play was taken out on tour and I was chosen to play Pinkie. My Aunt Judy went on the tour with me to act as my chaperone.

The *Coronet Christmas Chronicle* of 1909 said, "Look out for little Hermione Gingold who plays Pinkie. Will you ever see such delightful dancing, will any little girl of your acquaintance sing half so charmingly? Why half the West End and the whole of Kensingtonia will rave over the charming dancing of Pinkie."

My mother was close to achieving her nervous breakdown at last, but having only an audience of one (my sister Margaret), decided to postpone it until I was home again. After the tour, I returned to London and lessons with the governess.

This tedium was relieved by being engaged to alternate with Effie Byrne in playing the part of Falstaff's page, Robin, in *The Merry Wives of Windsor* back at His Majesty's Theatre again. Beerbohm Tree was a brilliant Sir John Falstaff but he was very old and becoming a little absentminded. In one scene, I had to announce: "My master, Sir John, is come in at your back door, Mistress Ford, and requests your company." Unfortunately, Beerbohm Tree hadn't come at all. Constance Collier, playing Mistress Ford, and I were left standing on the stage until he made a hurried appearance, not through the back door but through the huge fireplace!

I used to travel to the theatre by bus, and I was twelve years old when I fell in love with the bus conductor. To hear him shout "upstairs only" was, to my ears, sweeter than any music. I spent my entire theatre earnings on bus fares, travelling from Baker Street to the depot and from the depot to Baker Street. This went on for at least a month—until I encountered Pierre Dumont. He was the son of my French governess and the first foreign gentleman to come into my life, and oh, how foreign he turned out to be! If I shut my eyes tightly, I can see now how handsome he looked when he first opened the front door one windy afternoon as I arrived at Madame's house in Maida Vale.

Through meeting Pierre, I came to care more about my appearance. I brushed my hair and washed my nails, and the money I had hitherto spent on bus fares, I spent now in drenching myself with California Poppy and Phulnana perfume, until my father complained that our flat smelt like an Oriental bazaar.

Pierre brought to my notice the fact that there were forms of French literature other than the *Malheurs de Sophie*, and taught me to sing "Auprès de ma blonde".

31

I made such rapid strides with my French conversation that my mother was amazed though slightly surprised at the fact that I now spoke English with a French accent.

"If only you had made such progress with your German," she protested; but I hated my German governess. She lived with us and followed my sister and me everywhere—we called her "the spy". German lessons were just German lessons, while my French lessons were a pleasure. Then one day my mother said, "Hermione, I don't think that it is necessary for you to have any more French lessons."

She might as well have told me that the world was coming to an end. I cried and cried, and practically went into a decline—until another theatrical engagement effected an immediate recovery. Miss Ada Potter put on a play called *In the Name of the Tzar* at the Royalty Theatre. It was a strong dramatic piece and I had quite a large part as a poor peasant child.

N ext I was invited to understudy the leading child in the first production of *Where the Rainbow Ends* at the Savoy Theatre, with Charles Hawtrey directing. It was a charming children's fantasy play with flying carpets and lots of patriotism.

For me it was a heartbreaking engagement as I longed to play Rosamund and I never had the chance, as little Esmé Wynne was never once off, although I tried to push her downstairs several times.

Noël Coward was cast in the part of William, a page boy. He only had five lines but what he did with them was something quite fantastic. People used to stand and gape in astonishment. It was obvious the boy was destined to go far. Charles Hawtrey was

You could write the feelings of love I had for my mother on the head of a pin and still have room for the Lord's Prayer

Right: The photograph my mother feared would cause a scandal

Below: Father, German governess, Mother, Nurse, sister, Aunt, me with old bat

Pinkie and the Fairies, 1908. Miss Stella Patrick Campbell,
Marie Lohr, Ellen Terry, me at the end of the line

Hermione faces life

"Cry, Trojans, cry."
Cassandra in *Troilus and Cressida*,
Stratford-upon-Avon, 1912

Trapped in marriage

Eric Maschwitz, my second husband

Michael Joseph, my first husband

Optimism triumphs over experience

The Gate Revue, 1939. Gabrielle Brune, Michael Wilding,
me, Walter Crisham, Doris Gilmore, Jack McNaughton.
(Which one of us later married Elizabeth Taylor?)

''In the Rhine I was thrust,
Now I've rust on me bust.''
Sweet and Low, 1943

''I do miss Hermione badly.''
Sweet and Low, 1943

Exception to the Rule Britannia.
Sweeter and Lower, 1945

Sending up Robert Helpmann's Hamlet.
"I feel what it needs is a dash of
Sylphides, some Tchaikovsky and Margot
Fonteyn." *Sweeter and Lower*, 1945

Making up for "Borgia Orgy" with my dresser, Kitty.
Sweet and Low, 1943

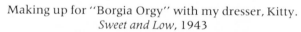

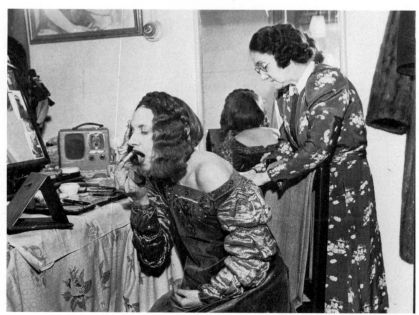

Monica Mallory, Olive Wright, Pam Trevers and me
in *Sweetest and Lowest*, 1946

"I've been painted by Picasso . . . from the
modern angle." *Sweetest and Lowest*, 1946

"That filly of fable, adorable Mabel,
the horse with the hansom behind."
Sweetest and Lowest, 1946

Returning to the Royal Garden
Party . . . with my invitation

Charles Hickman and Walter Crisham
outside my house, 81 Kinnerton Street

Inside
"Club 81".
Brian Hurst,
Alastair
Thompson,
Ilena Sylva,
Brian Michie,
Clarry Ashton,
Charles
Hickman,
Brenda Bruce,
Richard
Curnock,
Chris Hewett,
Joan Jefferson
Farjeon

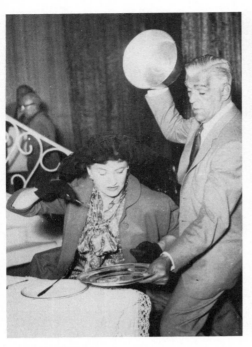

With Boris Karloff for *Night of a Hundred Stars*. "There's less in this than meats the eye."

Leaving England for America. This picture was faked.

I asked Charlie Chaplin, "Do you think I could find some Limelight in America?"

always threatening Noël with the sack but never carried out his threat because even Noël's scene-stealing had a ring of genius about it.

As children Noël and I were very friendly, yet as we got older, we weren't so close. When he became famous, he always seemed to be surrounded by a sycophantic mob calling him "the master" and positively kissing the chair he sat on. I was pleased at his well-deserved success but by then I liked to be the centre of attention myself.

A couple of times, young Noël came to tea in our flat. On one occasion, we made up a little play where we jumped off tables and chairs for effect and turned on all the taps in the flat to make the sound of a waterfall. When we tired of this game, we amused ourselves by sliding down the stairs on tea trays. This activity was not popular in a shared house and did the stair carpet no good at all. It was Noël's idea and when he left, my mother said, "You are never to ask that boy to tea again—he'll come to a bad end."

Noël also had the idea of putting on a revue. As far as I remember, he wrote it, directed it, and starred in it, even managing to persuade Charles Hawtrey to let him use the theatre. All we children were in the revue, as Noël's main objective was to make some money and he felt sure that our parents would pay to see their offspring perform. I can't recall what we all did in the show. I think we just sang an ensemble number at the beginning and at the end, while Noël showed off outrageously in the middle.

Our parents turned up in droves, but at the last minute, the London County Council forbade him to charge people to watch it. Noël didn't blink an eyelid. He took the money at the door as planned, then made the audience get up and leave and re-enter as his "free" guests. Now, a twelve-year-old child who can think up that way round regulations is obviously doomed to success.

When Noël and I were grown-up and met after long intervals in either London or New York, we always greeted each other with these words from *Where the Rainbow Ends*:

Now whosoever shall read this book, be they man, woman or child, shall find ere they close its pages the way to the land where the rainbow ends, for here where heaven kisses the earth, is found that fair city which some call "heart's content" and here all lost loved ones are found.

Then I'd say, "How are you? I haven't seen you for ages." And he'd say, "Fine," and everyone would look at us in amazement.

I was about thirteen when my mother decided Westcliff-on-Sea might be more conducive to her nervous breakdown than London, and she and I moved down there. I was sent to school at Southend College, where history repeated itself. I learnt nothing and cheated continuously but was kept on because of my appearance in the end-of-term plays. In truth, the only education an actress needs is to learn to write well enough to sign contracts.

My most memorable school performance was during fire-drill practice. We were supposed to slide down a linen shute to safety. It was such fun that I decided to prolong it by sticking my legs out in the middle. Pretending I was stuck, I assumed mock hysterics and started singing "Hark, Hark, the Lark" at the top of my voice, repeating it again and again until I was almost hoarse. No one could get me up or down.

The only thing I ever won at college was the three-legged race on Sports Day. I won because I cheated by kicking over the pair who should have won.

I still knew nothing of life. My mother had neglected to tell me I would soon become a woman, and I hadn't a clue where babies came from. The nearest she ever came to telling me the facts of life was the day she called me to her room and said she had something important to tell me. After a good deal of embarrassed coughing, she spluttered, "Don't ever sit down on a strange lavatory seat." The strain of imparting this information affected her so much that she had to retire to bed and I didn't see her for three days. I was more confused than ever.

My mother did, however, manage to make my existence miserable with other facts about life that I still follow. "Always," she said, "read the labels of medicine bottles and pills at least three times before you take them. Look in your food for needles and pins that the cook may have accidentally dropped in. Sheets on hotel beds are always damp, so unless you want to get rheumatism, sleep between the blankets. When you travel, always travel in the middle of the train—it's safer; and always sit near the exit in the cinema in case of fire."

My mother finally achieved her complete nervous breakdown and we returned to London. I was glad to be back in London and we must have been in the money again, for we moved into a large elegant flat off Manchester Square and I returned to my acting lessons. I studied hard and Miss Filippi told my mother she considered me to be the most promising dramatic actress of my class.

Then William Poel engaged me to play Cassandra in *Troilus and Cressida* at Stratford-upon-Avon. It was a marvellous production with Poel himself playing Pandarus. It was a curious production too, as several leading men's parts of generals, including Aeneas and Paris, were played by women. Thersites was played by Elspeth Keith, as Poel said, "If I cast a man he would be sure to overact."

I remember studying my part and wondering who was going to play Cressida: the beautiful Cressida, so beloved by Troilus. When we met for the first rehearsal, in walked a figure in a mackintosh and a homburg. I thought it might be the wardrobe mistress but, *no*, it was Edith Evans. She was playing the beautiful Cressida, although her face didn't seem to fit properly. I thought she'd have to use a lot of makeup, but how wrong I was. Miss Evans just sat in front of the mirror and said, "I'm beautiful, I'm beautiful," and she was. No makeup—just Christian Science.

I next went on to the Old Vic to play Jessica in *The Merchant of Venice*. I don't remember much about it except that Portia was played by Cathleen Nesbitt and the production was by Rosina Filippi. I do, however, remember Lilian Baylis and my first and last interview with her. She sent for me, and scared to death, I hurried into her office.

"Hermione," she said, "that wig of yours is an insult to the audience. Get rid of it."

"But, Miss Baylis," I said apologetically, "it's not a wig, it's my own hair!"

"I don't care," she said, banging the desk with her fist, "it goes back to the wigmaker in the morning!"

"Yes, Miss Baylis," I said. No one argued with her. Actors who asked her for a raise in salary were told, "I'll ask God, dear." Then she would shut her eyes, clasp her hands in prayer, and after a few minutes would smilingly say, "I'm sorry, dear, God says no."

After the performances at the Old Vic, the production went to Paris for a short season. It was my first trip outside England and although I was sixteen, my Aunt Judy again accompanied me as chaperone. I was thrilled and might have enjoyed the trip more if my mother hadn't warned me that I must on no account visit a French public convenience. She said these were very shocking places and forbade me to roam from the hotel or theatre. Foolishly, I obeyed her and subsequent trips have shown that for once her grim warnings had some justification.

Next came the First World War. That terrible war, supposed to be the war to end all wars, in which over four million servicemen lost their lives. Compared to the Second World War, I suppose the civilians had a relatively easy time, though the German zeppelin raids could be very frightening. In the first zep raid, my mother was terrified, but my father, sister, and I weren't scared at all. We thought it was great fun. We used to go down to shelter in the porter's flat because it was in the basement. Then one day, without warning, a zep raid occurred and a bomb dropped near enough to shake the whole building, whereupon my mother threw herself under the table and had hysterics. The next day, she left for Bournemouth, taking my sister with her. I stayed behind with my father because of my career—or that's what I told my mother. In reality it was because it would have been so boring being in Bournemouth with her.

My father was out a great deal because, in cahoots with a colonel whose name I forget—but it might have been Kerr—he invented the Kerrgold body belt. This was a belt worn around the waist that contained a sort of disinfectant and gave a complete protection against the fleas and lice that plagued our brave soldiers in the trenches. The government bought the Kerrgold body belt in great quantities and I suppose my father and the colonel could have made a small fortune if they'd wanted to. But not caring to profit from the war, they undersold them and my father ended the war practically broke again.

I enjoyed being on my own with my father. He'd opened an account for my mother and me at the new American department store in Oxford Street called Selfridges. I bought lots of material there, had some pretty clothes made up, and became what was known at the time as a flapper. I wore my long hair tied up with a large black bow, bought my first quite unnecessary "bust bodice", and began openly to use a little lip salve and papier poudré.

Also, I now had my first proper "boyfriend". His name was Leslie Hudson. I wasn't madly in love with him; I just loved him a little, in a friendly way. We had never been alone together without a chaperone. Even on the last evening we spent together before he went to the front, his mother was with us. She discreetly averted her eyes while he kissed me good-bye. Despite her presence, it was a long and passionate kiss of the sort I had never experienced before and I was terrified that I would have a baby.

After a week, I was so frightened that I forced myself to go to Bournemouth to tell my mother of the kiss. She said that as Leslie's mother had been there at the time, I would not have a baby. I went back to London relieved but none the wiser.

Poor Leslie. Months afterward, his mother arrived at our flat to tell me he'd been killed in action. I was devastated—it seemed such a dreadful waste.

The raids continued and they, at least, had their lighter side. The air-raid warnings used to be given by fat old policemen riding bicycles. They looked so funny blowing their whistles and shouting at us to take cover. After the raid was over, the policemen appeared again with placards on their backs that bore the magic words ALL CLEAR. I wondered why they didn't shout it and blow their whistles again. I came to the conclusion that, being old and fat, they were worn out from blowing and shouting before the raid!

Then one day, Leefe Robinson, a young pilot, got near enough to shoot down a zeppelin. London went wild and everybody was singing his praises—literally.

> And he brought a zep down
> At Cuffley and he won the VC
> So give him your kind applause.

That was the end of the zep raids but the war was not yet over. I seldom saw my father and was left to my own devices. Grown-up and yet not grown-up. How many of us are there who have not at some time or other passed through this state? Very few, I imagine. Then as my mother was pretty bored with her breakdown, she asked me to come and stay with her in Bournemouth.

It was there I met Michael Joseph, a young officer in the Machine Gun Corps. We met on the local ice-skating rink. Owing to my weak ankles, I was a very dangerous skater and it was my fault that I was bumped into, though it was his fault it kept being me he bumped into. One bump from Michael Joseph led to another and then to long country walks, stolen kisses, and romance as I'd never known it before. I lived in a state of unfulfilled bliss. I still had no idea what the details of the sex side of marriage were, but I was eager to find out and it was pure curiosity on my part that led to marriage. However, I did know that if one's mother wasn't present, marriage could somehow lead to babies. I told Michael that I would agree to marry him but only if he promised I should not have babies. He promised. I also explained that the most important thing in my life was my career and that I wanted to continue it. He agreed.

I went to Grantham, where he was stationed, to become Mrs Michael Joseph. On the morning of my wedding day, one of my aunts arrived looking very embarrassed. She had been sent by my mother to tell me the facts of life. To save her further embarrassment, I lied and told her I already knew them all. So she caught the next train for London, looking ten years younger.

It's a pity I spared her embarrassment, as I could have spared myself an unhappy marriage; for if I'd let her tell me what a wedding night entailed, I would certainly have cancelled the ceremony immediately.

After the wedding, we went to the local cinema, which was the only place open, for coffee and chocolate biscuits. My wedding night was spent in the local hotel in a rickety iron bed where, cuddling my teddy bear, I learned the facts of life. I was disappointed, tired, bored, and hurt. It's strange how little of my honeymoon I remember, which is probably just as well. All too soon, I started feeling sick and left for London, where I discovered to my horror, and to my mother's joy, I was going to have a baby. My mother was ecstatic and assured me I would love the baby when it arrived.

Michael's father was a diamond merchant in Hatton Garden and he and his wife lived in Stoke Newington, which was then a prosperous suburb. They were quite well off, but turned out to be a very dull Jewish family who were disappointed with Michael for marrying an actress. Michael and I were practically broke and though his parents could have helped us, they didn't. Mr Joseph gave me a gold cigarette case as a wedding present. As I was a non-smoker, it seemed at the time a rather useless present, but a trip to the pawnshop proved otherwise. Michael's parents also gave me a large diamond ring that found its way to the pawnbrokers, too.

When I had my first baby, I didn't know what was going to happen to me. I had a very kind and wonderful doctor, a sweet, caring nurse, and had the baby in my parents' home. I was not prepared for the pain and I screamed my head off.

"For a first baby, it was," the nurse told me, "an easy confinement." The doctor arrived in time to give me chloroform just before the baby was born. I was horrified and disgusted by the whole event.

I suppose I should have forgotten all this anguish when they placed the baby in my arms, but it didn't happen that way. I just said to the nurse, "Take it away." My mother said, "This sort of behaviour is not at all normal; you should be ashamed." But I wasn't.

I'd adopted a cat and though I'm reluctant to admit it, I think I loved the cat more than I loved the baby. On thinking it over, I feel sure it would have been different if my love for my husband hadn't worn a trifle thin.

We called the baby—a boy—Leslie in memory of Leslie Hudson, my first beau, who was killed in the war.

The war had ended and, with so many newly demobilised men trying to find work, Michael had a hard time finding a job. My father had disappeared again, leaving my mother out of funds, and it seemed I stood the best chance of getting employment. Consequently, within ten days of the baby's birth, I was up and about and going round the agents.

The agents sent me to Horsfield and Woodward, who sent out rather tatty tours. For want of anything better, I left the baby with my mother and Michael, and did several such tours. The one that sticks in my mind and that I had most fun in was *The Three Musketeers*. I played Constance and we played twice nightly. Once, by mistake, we were booked into a once-nightly theatre and panic broke out among our company. Knowing our show was too short, an early call was set in action to find out what other talents we had that could be used to lengthen the show. We found a conjurer, a dancer, and a female impersonator, and they were pressed unwillingly into service.

"I can sing," I said.

"Right," they said. "You sing then. What music have you got?"

"The only song I've got with me is 'The Willow Song' from *Othello*, which isn't suitable, I'm afraid; the words are quite unintelligible. For instance it starts, 'The poor soul sat sighing by a sycamore tree, sing all a green willow'."

"You could mumble the words a bit," they told me. So in the first act, softly and for no reason at all, as Constance I sang Desdemona's "Willow Song" with a blood-red spotlight on my face. I don't know what the audience thought of this mishmash but they didn't ask for their money back.

I was desperately unhappy. I found out that my marriage was a big mistake. I was paying too much for being curious. Michael took several ghastly ill-paid jobs with a series of weekly magazines while I tried to find us somewhere to live. Even in those days, it was difficult to find anywhere decent to live with practically no money. Eventually, I found a house in Lisson Grove, which was a pretty shady neighbourhood, meaning there were lots of trees for villains to lurk behind, but it was central and we could just about afford it. I pawned the few wedding presents that were left to buy us some basic furniture.

On Christmas Day, we went to Michael's parents for lunch. It was a foible of Mrs Joseph to fear that filling the Christmas pudding with traditional silver three-penny pieces might cause people to choke. Instead, she added some of the larger and much more valuable half-crowns. I had so many helpings of pudding that I looked and felt quite ill. Mrs Joseph feared I had swallowed a half-crown, but I had my collection of coins safely in my pocket. I was able to buy a new skirt, a table, and some things for the baby with the proceeds from that Christmas pudding.

Michael and I quarrelled a lot. He hated my beloved cat and when she had kittens, he rubbed a tiny kitten's nose in pepper for not using the garden. Clutching the tiny kitten who was sneezing and mewing, I rushed out of the house and went round to my mother who lived not far away. I told her that I would never go back to Michael. She was shocked at both Michael and me, and said, "Where will you go?" It was a question to which there was only one answer—*back*.

So back I went to my husband, and, funnily enough, years later Michael became a cat lover. He wrote a book about his Siamese cat that became a best-seller. So don't tell me that life isn't strange.

It seemed no time at all before I found myself pregnant again and no sooner was our next son, Stephen, born than I became pregnant a third time. In the very early morning of about my eighth month, I woke to discover I was haemorrhaging. I tried to wake Michael but he was a very deep sleeper. I promptly called my mother who was temporarily staying with us. She had hysterics, grabbed my hairbrush, and hit Michael with such force that it woke him up. We had no telephone, so I yelled out to him to go and get the doctor. Michael was sleepy, disagreeable, and uninterested. It was then that I said to myself, If I come through this, I'm going to leave him.

The doctor arrived and called an ambulance and I was taken to a nursing home where, after an agonising day and night in which I was really in danger of losing my life, I lost a stillborn baby girl.

By the time I left the nursing home and went back to Lisson Grove, Michael had at last found a job that suited him. It was a position with Hutchinson, the publishers, and carried a proper salary. He asked me to decide whether I would like a nurse or a servant. I couldn't have both, so I chose a nurse.

I was, I hate to admit, a terrible mother. I had no love for my babies, only a longing to get back to the theatre. I preferred doing the domestic work to looking after the babies, and after shopping, cooking meals, carrying coal up five flights of stairs, lighting fires, and cleaning, I had no time to look for work. Then, to make matters worse, my father turned up, smiling but penniless again, and he and my mother moved in with us.

My father and Michael got on splendidly and spent a lot of time together. I must say, to Michael's credit, he never grumbled once at their being part of our life. My mother and I, as usual, quarrelled. She thought I should give up the theatre and concentrate on the children, and I couldn't listen to her advice however loudly she gave it. I can hear her now. "Hermione," she pleaded, "do give up the theatre, then you could devote yourself to learning the harp or bowling."

Michael became publicity manager at Hutchinson, later joined Curtis Brown, the literary agents, and then went on to found his own immensely successful publishing house, which he named after himself.

We were still desperately short of funds and Michael found he could make extra money on the side by reading manuscripts, being paid a tiny sum for each manuscript he read and summarised. He brought the fruits of potential authors home and I helped swell our income by reading them, too. Through necessity, I acquired the knack of reading very quickly. I can still absorb books and scripts pretty fast, so I suppose I have one thing for which to thank Michael. One week Michael brought home a great pile of short stories; these were, for the most part, so badly written that Michael sat down and wrote a book that was published under the title *Short Story Writing for Profit*—and it made *him* quite a profit.

The extra money we earned manuscript reading meant I could give up some of my domesticity and try to get back into the theatre, but by now it seemed any reputation I had built up as an actress was forgotten. There seemed to be no hope left in my life and certainly no romance, at least not in Lisson Grove. I am an incurable romantic and it is difficult for me to live in a world without romance.

Relations with Michael became more and more strained. I couldn't sleep with him because I was afraid of having another baby. In those days, there was no pill and no coils; these goodies were not with us yet. I know this sounds ridiculous, but Michael and I simply had no idea where to get advice on how to stop babies coming. Sex and contraception just weren't talked about by respectable married couples.

I tried to help Michael at Hutchinson by organising a literary tea and it was there, across the teacups, that I met a young man who also worked at Hutchinson. His name was Eric Maschwitz and he was to become my second husband.

E ric was full of charm and wit and embodied all the romance I so lacked in my unhappy life with Michael. Eric invited me to a grand birthday party he was giving himself in a big house belonging to a friend. I managed to make myself a black taffeta frock and though I say it myself, I looked rather special. I've never been pretty, but I am special. It worked like a charm on Eric!

Meanwhile back at Lisson Grove, things weren't going well at all. Michael wasn't earning enough for our upgoing lifestyle. We now had a maid as well as a nurse and we still had my parents living with us.

After a while, we decided to do a moonlight flit from Lisson Grove. We left everything in the house except our clothes and babies' cribs. We intended to pay the rent—it was very overdue and we just wanted to have time to do so. So we moved to Dorset Square.

Eric phoned me constantly and sent me books and gramophone

records, and one day I went to his flat in Bloomsbury, where we made love. I've just finished reading his autobiography in which he says he only took the flat in order to make love to me. He really was a wonderful lover and with him I had my first orgasm.

I couldn't bear going back to Michael who, for some reason, didn't want me to leave him. He decided to take a cottage at Seaview on the Isle of Wight for the summer. We left London, taking the children, the maid, and the nurse. He was suspicious about Eric and was madly jealous. I warned Eric not to write to me while I was away as Michael would be sure to open all my letters, but Eric did write. He addressed his letters to the maid but in his own handwriting, and the fat was in the fire!

Michael carried me upstairs to our bedroom and beat me black and blue with a wooden curtain rod. Then he got a razor and said, "I'm going to kill you." I knew that if I showed that I was frightened, he would have, so I said, "Don't be silly," and he slammed out of the room, locking the door behind him. I found my handbag with just enough money in it to get me back home, so I climbed out of the window and caught the ferry and then the train to London. I was frightened Michael might try and follow me, so I sat in a "ladies only" carriage. Just as the train was about to leave, five nuns suddenly entered my compartment and I was trapped with them all the way to London. I couldn't sit still for very long as my derrière hurt so much from Michael's beating and all I wanted to do was to howl my eyes out at the mess I was making of my life, but there I was, surrounded by five silent, self-disciplined nuns. It was a tough journey.

In London I went to stay with sympathetic aunts. Eric arrived and we decided to elope to the South of France. I had no clothes, but Eric got in through the back window at Dorset Square to get me some. My father, despite his friendship with Michael, was wonderful. He came to the station to see us leave on the boat train, brought me chocolates and magazines for the journey, and waved us good-bye as off we went into the sunset, romance rearing its fragile head once more.

We eventually ended up at Cagnes-sur-Mer, which is a delightful old Grimaldi stronghold perched high on a hill above Cannes, and we managed to get the only villa with running water and a proper lavatory. This completely fascinated the children of Cagnes-sur-Mer, and the younger ones came and asked whether they could pull the plug.

The kitchen was sort of a cave under the house where a very old Canneoise prepared miracles of food for us. I never went down there after my first visit because I didn't think I'd like what I saw. I may have a lot of foreign blood but the English in me calls for a clean kitchen and a clean-handed cook. We kept a goat that she milked and Eric bought a donkey called Nanette and a little canary-coloured cart for her to pull me about in. Once a week, we all danced on the gravel in the square while the band played tunes that were so old that they were new to me.

The Grimaldi castle had a large tree, about forty feet tall, growing in the courtyard. It commanded a view over the whole countryside and seemed unreal. Now I hear the Americans have invaded Cagnes. They're still dancing, but a dance floor has been put down in the square and a modern dance band plays. The Grimaldi château has been made into a museum, and there's a proper drainage system in the town. "You can't hold back progress," I say to myself. Sometimes I wish you could. Needless to say, I've never been back and all this is purely what "they" tell me. Some of my best friends feature in this book as "they", and they can be relied upon to tell it like it is.

The only drawback to living in Cagnes was the scorpions. Every morning I had to shake out my shoes before putting them on. I consider myself an animal lover but I'd squash a scorpion anytime, saying, "Good riddance to bad rubbish"—a saying much used in pubs, especially when some obvious lady of the night gets up and leaves.

It would have taken more than a few scorpions to mar our bliss. While Eric pretended to write a novel, we planned our future, swam, played tennis, rode in our donkey cart—or rather pushed and pulled the obstinate beast—and made love in the moonlight under the orange trees. Eric had told me he knew how to prevent babies and I believed him until I found I was pregnant again. I left Eric to settle things up and I went back to London. My Aunt Hannah, who now owned a very chic nursing home, took me in. As I couldn't keep any food down, a curettage was easy to arrange.

Eric rejoined me in London and we moved in together. He resigned from Hutchinson, as to carry on working with my husband Michael had an air of impropriety about it.

Although we never seemed to have any money, we were divinely happy. I managed to get back into the West End again, playing Liza in *If* and then Maudie, the old woman, in *The Dippers*. They weren't very good parts but at least I was in the theatre again and my earnings kept the wolf from the door.

Somehow we managed to live quite a grand life. We ate at the Café Royal a lot and met masses of interesting people—Rebecca West, Ronald Firbank, and others it would be too snobbish to mention. As well as being loved, I was being educated. I began to read Marcel Proust instead of Elinor Glyn.

Eric finished writing his novel and I got a job to go on tour with a play called *Within the Law*. I managed to fix a job for Eric as assistant stage manager to the company and off we went for three months. We were so much in love that even the worst of our theatrical digs seemed paradise.

When the tour ended, I had a confrontation with Michael, who offered to take me back as a wife if I would give up not only Eric but also the theatre. I refused his offer and he divorced me. He asked me whether I wanted the children and I said no, he was welcome to them, but I'd like my cat.

I didn't see my children again until they were grown-up. Leslie was sixteen when I received a telegram from Michael saying our elder son was dangerously ill. Previously, Leslie had been playing cricket at boarding school and had received a severe blow on the head from a cricket ball and had now developed a brain tumour as a result of the accident. Michael's telegram said that Leslie should have the tumour removed but that the operation was not only dangerous but very expensive and he couldn't afford it.

Where doctors and medical treatment are concerned, I always believe in getting the best, so I made inquiries and found that the leading brain surgeon in the country was a Professor Cairns. I went to see him and he agreed to operate on Leslie immediately. The operation was a complete success. I had been such a terrible mother that I was glad to have a chance to do something to help. It was probably the only good thing I ever did for my child.

As soon as Michael's divorce from me was absolute, both Eric's mother and mine descended upon us and demanded that Eric and I should marry. Neither of us wanted to, but the sight of both our mothers in tears was not to be borne. So, as I clutched a penny bunch of violets, we got married at the registry office in Marylebone. I remember the look of surprise on the kindly old gentleman's face when, after he married us, I said, "Thank you very much and I do hope I'll see you again soon . . ."

Married—and that was the beginning of the end. We thought that as we weren't living anywhere in particular, and certainly not in sin anymore, we'd better find a home.

After a brief search, I found a divine little house in Pembroke Walk Studios. It was a former artist's studio with a bedroom on a balcony, a living room thirty feet high, and a little garden. Michael sent round my cat and life was bliss.

We were practically broke but as Eric was walking down the Strand one afternoon, he bumped into Lance Sieveking. Eric mentioned he was out of work and Lance said, ''Why don't you come and work with me at the BBC?'' It was as simple as that. In those days, the BBC wasn't considered a fit job for a man, but Eric and I were delighted. When Eric got his first paycheque and came home carrying a box of groceries, I burst into tears of happiness.

Broadcasting was really in its infancy and still in its first venue at Savoy Hill, off the Embankment. The BBC sent Eric to present outside broadcasts; I remember him covering the boat race and the return of Amy Johnson, the aviatrix, at Hendon Aerodrome. He also kept writing scripts that he sold to the BBC under the nom de plume Holt Marvell.

One of these was a musical called *Goodnight Vienna*. The film director Herbert Wilcox knew that it was really Eric who had written it and he rang up the morning after it was broadcast offering Eric two hundred pounds to buy the film rights. We were delighted with the deal until the film was produced. It was the first British talking musical, starred Anna Neagle and Jack Buchanan, and it made a fortune. However, Eric didn't do badly out of *Goodnight Vienna* as it had a long West End run and went out on numerous tours. Towards the end of one of these tours, the show began to get a little tired and was playing in Huddersfield, Yorkshire, to not very good audiences. Eric asked the theatre manager, ''How are they liking it?'' The manager replied, ''About as much as they'd like a musical called *Goodnight Huddersfield* in Vienna.''

Eric was doing well at the BBC. When they discovered he'd worked in publishing, they promoted him to work on the *Radio Times*. Within months the *Radio Times* editor died and Eric was named his successor. Life seemed too good to be true. It was.

I got a job too and went off on a short tour as understudy in a play called *Lido Lady*. The General Strike of 1926 made a slight hiccup in the tour. For a few days, all buses and trains came to a grinding halt. Our audiences slumped a little, but volunteers stepped in to move food supplies and man the transport. The *Lido Lady* company travelled to its next venue on a bus driven by a medical student, and the strike was broken soon after.

A little later, the trains were back to normal, and as we were playing near London, I asked the stage manager whether I could go home on Sunday and return to the show on Monday. I was given permission and rushed home on the last train after the Saturday-night performance to surprise Eric.

I tiptoed up to the balcony. I needed no light—only the moon—to show me Brian Michie, a mutual friend of ours, asleep in *our* bed. I shook him awake.

"What are you doing here?" I asked. "Where's Eric?"

Brian looked embarrassed and mumbled, "Well—er—he's with a friend."

"A woman?"

"I'm afraid so."

With these words, the bottom fell out of my life. Despite my experience with Michael, up until that moment I was still naive enough to believe that true love and lasting commitment did exist and that I could find them with Eric. I collapsed in a bewildered heap and Brian made things worse by suggesting I hop into bed with him. I slapped his face and wept.

"How could he do this to me?"

"Easily I'm afraid, dear. That's how he's made. Come to bed now."

"Get out! Get out!" I yelled. "I never want to see you again!"

He dressed and went out into a rainy morning dawn. I flung myself on the bed and cried myself to sleep. When I woke, it was ten-thirty and Eric appeared with a cup of tea for me. I didn't know what to say, but he did.

"Don't hate me," he said.

"I can't help it. I'm leaving you," I said.

"Don't go please. I don't want you to go."

"I wish I was dead," I sobbed.

"Don't overact, dear. Stop crying. Get up. Do your hair. And get yourself a lover."

"You don't mean it?"

"I do. Get yourself a lover."

For me, that was the end of our marriage. I was so unhappy that when I went back to the show, I took his advice and went to bed with the no-good leading man.

It emerged that Eric had been sleeping not only with my cousin but also with one of my girl friends. I never had many girl friends, but I did have one that I liked very much. I had asked her to dinner to meet Eric and the next thing I knew was that he'd got her pregnant and was asking me whether I knew where she could get an abortion. That was the end of my friendship with her and the start of my lasting decision never to have any girl friends. There was one exception to this rule and she makes an appearance much later in this tell-all.

I don't want to alienate half my readers, but to be honest, I find that women who tend to be brilliant career women reduce me to awed silence; that housewives speak practically a foreign language; and that actresses only want to talk about themselves, and that's precisely what I want to do.

However, I do feel women are here to stay. Also, I'm delighted England has a woman Prime Minister. I wish America would elect a woman President. With women in charge, I'm practically certain we would never again be plunged into a world war. Fighting is essentially a masculine idea—a woman's weapon is her tongue.

I once said, "There are far too many men in politics and not enough elsewhere." Someone thought to put it into the *Penguin Book of Quotations*, probably because they knew it was true. The other truism of mine in that volume is: "What Americans call cross-ventilation, the English call draughts."

I went back to Pembroke Walk Studios after the tour. Eric was seldom there but was always very kind and attentive, although when I asked him whether he wanted a divorce, he replied, "No, on no account." Not very sporting, but then I felt the same way because I was afraid (so was he, it turned out) that we'd be trapped into marriage once again. He now had a rather grand new job as director of BBC's Light Entertainment, and so we decided to move, but with the proviso that separate bedrooms were now a requirement. We found a charming ground floor and basement flat with a garden in a house in Edwardes Square.

Broadcasting's popularity was growing fast; television didn't exist yet, of course, but listeners were becoming quite enthusiastic about radio drama. I was cast in several plays and became something of a regular. The BBC employed me to play everything from straight dramatic roles to singing the laughing song from *Die Fledermaus*. Early radio was great fun! The studios at Savoy Hill contained occasional tables and armchairs and had framed oil paintings on the walls; they seemed more like drawing rooms with microphones in the middle. For evening broadcasts, artists were expected to wear full evening dress even though no one was going to see them!

Two productions I was in were considered radio landmarks. One was Compton Mackenzie's *Carnival*. It was directed by Sir John Gielgud's brother Val, and starred Compton himself, Lillian Harrison, Harmon Grisewood, and had two orchestras. All radio broadcasts were live in those days and the evening it was broadcast, Savoy Hill was in chaos because we used every studio.

The other memorable landmark was a strange morality tale called *Kaleidoscope*, broadcast in 1929. It was written and directed by Lance Sieveking who said it was "a play too purely radio to be printed for reading". Nowadays people would say "So what?" but in those simple times people were amazed and everyone who possessed a crystal set put on their headphones and twisted their "cat's whisker" to tune into *Kaleidoscope*. I played the wife who was one of the six principals, but there were over one hundred in the cast, for the large crowd scenes had to be played then and there with a live crowd in the studios. The next morning, the newspapers acclaimed the production, saying, "Real wireless drama at last."

Wireless—I loved that misnomer. The corners of London sitting rooms would contain a vast array of cables, leads, and paraphernalia, and the popular music hall joke of the times was "What's all that wire for?" "Wireless, you fool!"

One piece of inspired casting was to ask me to play Mary Magdalene in *The Man Born to Be King*. I actually played her rather well. I remember the cast wasn't allowed to have their names listed in the *Radio Times* as it was considered blasphemous.

I loved doing radio dramas, but as Eric rose through the BBC ranks, it became harder for me to do them. Other members of the cast would see me in the studio and say, "Oh, you're in this, are you? Yes, well, of course, your husband is Light Entertainment Director, isn't he?" Even if they didn't say it, I felt they were thinking it; and although I knew I'd got the job on my own merit only because I was a good actress, it made me feel uncomfortable.

In another play, I was a bullfrog. The BBC had no library of recorded sound effects then and when the director asked, "How can we make the background noise of a bullfrog in the next scene?" I said, "I'll have a go." All I had to do was croak, and I was sent down to the basement and told to start croaking when the green light went on. Unfortunately, no one switched the light off. I thought perhaps the play was overrunning and I carried on croaking for about three-quarters of an hour until someone came down and asked me what on earth I was doing. I always carry on until I'm told to stop.

One of my greatest radio thrills was when, being the only actress in one production who could play the piano, I was asked whether I'd play the first eight bars of "Jesu Joy of Man's

Desiring". I was practising the piece when two engineers came in, saying, "Oh, no—this piano isn't good enough to give a recital on; you should go upstairs to the Bechstein." They thought I was a real concert pianist and I was delighted.

I also wrote several plays for the BBC. The best-received was called *Tickets, Please*. It was about a theatrical company that got stranded on tour by the management and put on a show at the railway station to be allowed to board the train home.

Sir John Reith was the BBC's formidable general manager, as the director general was then called, and Denis Freeman was head of Drama. Denis used to do some quite exciting and avant-garde plays, including one called *Les Mariés de la Tour Eiffel* by Jean Cocteau, in which I played the part of a telegram. The play was scored for two whips, a washboard, a whistle, and an iron that was banged down on a piece of tin. Rehearsals were going splendidly, if noisily, when suddenly Sir John walked in and said, "What is this?" Looking round at the whip and washboard, he asked, "Is this supposed to go on the air?"

"Oh, yes," said Denis. "It's a play by Jean Cocteau."

"It is *not* going on the air," said Sir John, and walked out. That was the end of that.

In another play, I invented the character of a cat, and here I encountered Sir John's rigorous censorship. I wanted to say "the cat sat in the tree and spat defiance". A memo came saying the audience might find the word *spat* offensive and I must alter it to "hissed" defiance. How times have changed.

My most risqué radio part was a comedy character I invented called Mrs Pullpleasure. She wasn't a lady of pleasure at all, quite the opposite. She was the sort of lady who eats half a banana and wraps the remaining half carefully into its skin to save for later. I recreated her subsequently onstage and did just that. She was a depressingly downbeat grey lady, which is why I called her Mrs Pullpleasure.

In those days, the BBC was small enough for Sir John to exert an eagle-eyed one-man censorship, and the growth of the BBC and its bureaucracy didn't improve things. In 1947, I had an almighty and rather public row with them. I had recorded a radio revue called *Now Is the Time*. The BBC censored some of the items from the show, including a six-minute dialogue based on Dorothy Parker's short story "Here We Are", which couldn't have been more innocent. They asked me to rerecord the programme, I refused and they had to cancel the broadcast. GINGOLD MAKES A STAND AGAINST THE BBC, said the newspaper headlines. I was pretty cross and explained, "My show is extremely sophisticated and not like most BBC music-hall programmes, which are vulgar in the worst possible way." I received hundreds of letters in support, but the BBC was furious and threatened never to employ me again.

Our row was a contributory factor to leading Lord Reith to produce his famous *Green Book*, which he brought out in 1949. This was a top-secret policy guide for BBC writers and producers. It firmly said, "There can be no compromise with doubtful material. It must be cut." It went on to say:

> There is an absolute ban upon the following:
> Jokes about—
> > Lavatories
> > Effeminacy in men
> > Immorality of any kind
> Suggestive references to—
> > Honeymoon couples
> > Chambermaids
> > Fig leaves
> > Ladies underwear, e.g., "winter draws on"
> > Animal habits, e.g., rabbits
> > Lodgers
> > Commercial travellers.

Of revue and cabaret, he said, "A great deal of material performed elsewhere in those types of entertainment is just not suitable to be broadcast."

When I think of how immaculately clean we had to be and

what they get away with nowadays! I may sound old-fashioned, but I think things have gone too far now. I've always preferred subtlety to crudity—although you may not think it from this book. Double entendre is a different matter. I love jokes where people can take one meaning or another to suit themselves.

It was during a radio play being directed by Tyrone Guthrie that I met Peter Hannen. He was up at Cambridge but it was his vacation and he had come to swell the numbers in the play's crowd scenes. There were no Equity Actors Union regulations in those days to prevent Tyrone using his friends to make up the crowd.

Peter was handsome, young, charming, and we both fell in love—luckily, with each other. Peter's father was a well-known actor named Nicholas Hannen who for years had lived with Athene Seyler. As far as I was concerned, she had nothing to recommend her except the fact that she was a brilliant actress.

I was never asked to their house, but I couldn't have cared less. Peter and I lived in a fantasy world of our own. Even though Eric and I were still living together in Edwardes Square, we had our separate bedrooms, and Peter spent some nights in mine, which didn't bother Eric at all as he was involved with Lady R. W. (who shall remain nameless).

After the play was over, Peter and I went to Italy and stayed on Lake Maggiore in a small village on the unfashionable side of the lake. We rented a dear little house and an Italian maid who couldn't speak a word of English. Peter found a secluded cove round the bay from the village, where we used to swim in the nude. We were madly in love and even made love under the waters of Lake Maggiore. After a few days, we began to notice little groups of rowing boats encircling our cove. Each day they seemed to come closer and appeared to be watching us swim. Then they complained to the mayor, who sent us a letter asking us to refrain from nude bathing as it overexcited the locals. When we next swam, we wore our swimsuits; the mayor was delighted and the locals pretended they were, too.

I don't think I've ever been happier than I was with Peter in those sun-filled days on Lake Maggiore. I should have known it couldn't last.

When we got back to London, I found I was pregnant again and went into a nursing home to have a curettage. While I was recovering, Peter visited me every day, and rightly so, as it was his baby. On the day I was to leave the nursing home, he told me that Athene Seyler had said she would get him a part in a play with Diana Wynyard if he gave me up. I was stunned that he should even consider it, but he did and left. I think I cried as many tears as there is water in Lake Maggiore. At least it felt like it. I didn't even stop for meals. I wanted to die, I loved Peter so much. He was the real love of my life.

Eric put up with my tears for long enough and I certainly can't blame him for sending me to stay with Val Gielgud and his wife, who were neighbours and kind and patient. I tried to forget Peter and I know that when I got back to Edwardes Square, I tore up his photographs and burnt his letters. I then had several short-lived affairs with men I didn't care for in the hope I would forget him.

Years later Athene Seyler and I both had cameo parts in a film of Dickens's *The Pickwick Papers*. We had no scenes together, which was probably fortunate for all concerned.

Eric decided it would be better if we left Edwardes Square and lived separately—but, if possible, near each other. In spite of the fact our marriage was over, we were still great friends. We eventually found two adjoining flats in the Adelphi where we could lean out of the window to talk to one another. We used to wave to each other every morning and evening. I decorated my own flat and then Eric's. I must say they were both charming.

If I have been hard on Eric, I didn't mean to be. In retrospect, he was just weak about wine and women. He wrote several novels and the lyrics of "These Foolish Things", "Room Five-Hundred-and-Four" and "A Nightingale Sang in Berkeley Square", as well as a number of successful musicals. I remember rushing from the BBC, where I was doing a radio play, to His Majesty's Theatre in the Haymarket to catch the final curtain on the first night of *Balalaika*. I discovered Eric standing at the back of the orchestra, shouting "Author, Author", and having started it off, rushing round to take a bow.

Balalaika was a great success and Eric took his current girl friend to a villa in Juan les Pins to relax. When he left Juan les Pins, he gave me the keys to the villa and I went down there with a new boyfriend, Anthony. The villa belonged to a retired major who had been stationed in India most of his life. It was full of brass, animals' heads, and spears. Very unsuitable for the South of France.

At that time, there seemed to be very little nightlife in Juan les Pins, so Anthony and I thought we'd go to the cinema *bleu* at the local brothel. I'd never seen a blue film before and was very curious. We were shown into a room with cushions on the floor that seemed to be occupied by several stony-faced English travel agents who'd come to see whether it was bad enough for their clients to be sent to. Well, I don't know what decision they arrived at, but it turned out to be incredibly funny. It was called *The Violin Lesson*, and all the ladies were dressed in Louis XVI costumes with ill-fitting wigs that tipped over their faces every time they changed position. Anthony and I laughed as it became apparent that none of them would ever give Yehudi Menuhin the slightest competition. We laughed so much that the madam came and asked us to leave because we were spoiling the evening for the other guests; so we left. But first we thanked her and told her how much we'd enjoyed ourselves.

When we made love that night, it was impossible not to be

59

reminded of *The Violin Lesson* and we laughed and laughed. Really, sex and laughter do go very well together, and I wondered —and still do—which is the more important.

Anthony had to return to England, but I stayed on a little longer and while I was lying on the beach one day, a beautiful English boy came over and said, "I've been watching you for some time and liked what I saw. I notice you didn't speak French—are you English?"

"As the White Cliffs of Dover," I replied, and that was the beginning of a long love affair.

His name was Leslie Bradley. He was very handsome and very mysterious. All I could find out about him was that he came from Paris, where he had been employed by Cole Porter—as what, I don't know. He told me he was into Indian philosophy and often left his body and went to visit his mother in London, which reminded me that I should return to London and get on with my career. Leslie went with me—both of us by train.

Shortly after we returned, my darling father died. He seemed as spry as ever and in the best of health when he contracted pneumonia as a result of sitting in an open-air racing car with his cousin during a rainstorm. He was convinced champagne would cure him, but he died within a matter of days. It was a terrible shock to me and life without him has never seemed quite the same.

My career was going slowly. I did several plays, mostly understudying the leading lady, but down the road from my Adelphi flat was a tiny theatre club called the Gate. As it was a club, it wasn't subject to the usual censorship regulations and they could put on foreign or unusual plays that otherwise wouldn't have been seen. Eugene O'Neill's *Desire Under the Elms* and Lillian Hellman's *The Children's Hour* had their British premieres at the Gate.

The Gate Theatre was run in those days by a wonderful director named Peter Godfrey, and everyone was paid the same salary —three pounds a week. One went from walk-on to star parts to sometimes serving coffee and cake in the bar. There were only two dressing rooms, one for men and one for women. Among the actors and actresses I remember working there were Flora Robson, who was sensitive and businesslike and played strong dramatic roles; Stewart Granger, who was charming and never seemed to take life seriously; Elsa Lanchester, whose recent autobiography I enjoyed a lot and inspired me to get on with this book; Michael Wilding; James Mason, who even then had his delicious rasping voice; and Vivien Leigh, whose fragile beauty I tried to emulate until Michael Wilding told me everyone was saying I looked as if I had a toothache.

I played all sorts of parts, from Lily Malone in *Hotel Universe* to Vidette in *I Hate Men*. The chief hater in *I Hate Men* was Margaret Rawlings, but Robert Helpmann was also in it and we both agreed it was a very curious title. That production was the start of my long friendship with Robert Helpmann, who had just arrived from Australia and was making his first British appearance. Robert was known to his friends as Bobby, but how he came by this amusing nickname, I have never been able to discover.

When Bobby and I reminisced, we wondered how the Gate managed to stage *I Hate Men*, for on that tiny stage, the sets included a box at the opera, a yacht at sea, and the exterior of a French café where Bobby played the waiter in a house of ill fame. In all, there must have been about twelve different scenes—a Drury Lane production on a stage the size of an average sitting room.

In *Little Lord Fauntleroy*, I played Dearest; Elsa Lanchester played Little Lord Fauntleroy; and Alan Napier played the Earl of Dorincourt.

61

Elsa was very versatile, and I remember how poignantly she sang "Don't Sell No More Drink to My Father" in *Ten Nights in a Bar Room*—so much so that several drunken members of the audience were reduced to tears. I also remember that she borrowed my only pair of satin lace drawers, as after the show she said she was going out with a talented young character actor, Charles Laughton. I don't remember whether she ever gave them back to me, but she married Charles Laughton and I feel partly responsible.

I loved the variety and fun of working at the Gate, but then it closed temporarily and I did a couple of straight plays at the "Q" Theatre. Then Denis Freeman gave me a part in Herbert Farjeon's new revue, *Spread It Abroad*, at the Saville Theatre. It was my first real London revue. Dorothy Dickson, Ivy St Helier, and Nelson Keys were the stars, but I was in some nice numbers, including a song with Dorothy and Ivy called *Follow the Daughter*. Here I played the Prime Minister's daughter, Ishbel Macdonald. In another good sketch, I was an exhausted cockney bicycle racer who was called upon to make a speech. The critics noticed me favourably, especially in a skit set in a theatre foyer where Lyle Evans and I played avid first-night theatregoers.

Walter Crisham was also in the revue; he and I were to work together on and off for the next ten years. Wally was an American and very debonair; he also had a heart of gold that he kept camouflaged under a cloak of rudeness and smart taunts. Although he was very handsome, he always looked as if he was about to say something libellous—and he usually did. After rehearsing with Wally for a few days, I felt quite capable of singing in a cage with a wild tiger; and in later days, Norman Marshall would often rehearse our duets, defending himself with a chair.

Spread It Abroad also contained the first performance of Eric's song "These Foolish Things Remind Me of You". Eric always told me he'd written the song about me. They were beautiful lyrics and I was very touched until I heard he'd told the actress Anna May Wong he'd written it about her. You see I know all about men. In spite of this, I like them enormously.

Leslie Bradley was still living with me. He was a wonderful antidote to Peter, but he had no sense of humour and to live with me without quarrelling, humour is essential. We ended our affair with a silly row about—well, it was so silly I forget what it was about. He left unwillingly and took a room in the neighbourhood in case I changed my mind and wanted him back. If I hadn't been working, I might have.

I was doing the revue at night and radio plays for the BBC in the daytime and I was too exhausted to do more than climb up to my flat on the top floor before falling into bed.

My mother appeared to have taken my father's death remarkably well. She was living in London but didn't often visit me because of all the stairs, and I didn't blame her. One special day, she came to lunch and I cooked a very English meal consisting of steak and kidney pudding and trifle. I made the steak and kidney pudding myself because my daily maid didn't cook what she called "common food".

Just as we were sitting down, the telephone rang and it was Eric. He sounded grim and not without reason.

"Peter Hannen died this morning and I wanted to tell you before you read it in the papers." Peter had been filming *The Water Babies* and after being immersed in cold river water for hours on end, he'd caught a kidney infection.

I went into the bedroom and locked my door and cried and cried. I realised that in spite of everything, I still loved Peter. My mother knocked on the door and said, "Come out and have some lunch; it will do you good."

"Peter, I love you and I always will. You are too young to die—and my mother thinks steak and kidney pudding would do me good!" I wouldn't answer her and spent all day in my locked bedroom crying. I couldn't stop. My mother went home; and the steak and kidney pudding was given to the cat.

Eric knew how much I had loved Peter and he tried to console me with an invitation to join him in Budapest. He was there looking for an actress for his new musical *Magyar Melody*. He wanted a Hungarian beauty who could play the violin, sing, act, and speak English. He found it quite difficult. Violin, yes. Sing, yes. English, no. Act, no. As it looked as if he might be spending the rest of his life in Budapest, he said it would do me good to come for a holiday.

So off to Paris I went to board the Orient Express, a train full of elegance, glamour, and orchids. Passengers sipped champagne and changed into full evening dress to eat a six-course meal, served by white gloved waiters, while a pianist tried to drown out the train's rattling as we sped across Europe into Hungary. It was a divine trip marred only by the fact that they served sterilised milk with the coffee; but I dare say it's not the only time sterilisation has been used to overcome a difficulty.

When we arrived in Budapest, I thought I heard music, and, sure enough, when I got off the train I was met by a gypsy band. The leader handed me a bouquet of red roses and wanted me to sit on a luggage truck while the gypsies played "Csak egy Kislany van a vilagon. . . ."

I wonder what would have happened if the station had been Waterloo. They would probably all have been arrested for creating a disturbance. I could picture a British policeman saying, "Move along, you gypsies, you can't play here." Eric appeared. "You arranged this, of course," I said, and started to act the star. I was hauled off the luggage truck, bowing graciously from left to right while the gypsies played "Voros bort ittam az este, ragyogo csillagom galambom. . . ." It really was a grand exit.

In Budapest Eric had taken an enormous villa on the Rue Callahagy. He was determined that I should enjoy myself and I did. I met two charming American boys and while Eric was busy auditioning actresses, I and the two Americans spent most of our time at the swimming pool in the St Gelet Hotel, which boasted real waves and a very chic English clientèle.

There were rumours of war in the air, but no one seemed to worry about them. In fact, I was having such a lovely time that when Eric had to go back to England, I decided to stay on.

In May 1938, Hitler marched into Austria, which felt uncomfortably close to Hungary, and I began to feel I, too, should return home. I tried to get a seat on a train but all the other English tourists seemed to have had the same idea and I was told it would be weeks before I could buy a ticket. I went to the British Embassy, explained the situation, and dropped a few names —including that of my friend Admiral Hugh Sinclair, head of Naval Intelligence—then I returned to the villa to wait. That evening I received a message to say I could leave the next day. I packed and the following morning I was escorted to the station by a huge plainclothesman who looked like a prizefighter. He led me to a couchette and stood guard outside the carriage until the train started. The train took me to France and the boat train to England, where I felt considerably safer than I had in Budapest. The feeling wasn't to last long.

One morning I leaned out of my window to tell Eric that I was leaving my Adelphi flat, as I had found a beautiful little cottage in Marylebone, off Wigmore Street.

The cottage was unique. It was quite large with two bedrooms, a sitting room, and dining room. At one time, it had been the blacksmith's forge of Marylebone. It was built around a courtyard and what remained of the forge next door still shod the occasional horse. It was in the heart of London and yet from the outside it still remained an old black-and-white cottage. I filled the courtyard with tubs of flowers—which every so often got eaten by one of the horses. Inside with its whitewood panelling, open fireplace, white muslin curtains, and Staffordshire china, it looked quite charming. I remember getting William Chappell, the stage designer, to paint a mural in the dining room, and my maid's horror when she told me, "There's a young man painting the dining room wall with a very small paintbrush—he won't half take a time!"

I loved that cottage dearly. It was a historic piece of London that should have been preserved as a national monument—and not just because I'd lived there. But they pulled it down just as they pulled down most of Adam's beautiful Adelphi.

When the Gate Theatre reopened in 1939, Norman Marshall had taken it over and to open the new season, he decided to put on a revue, getting good writers to contribute and comment on present happenings. Satire was to be the mainstay of this new sort of entertainment. As I was the only member of the Company who could sing, I was to be, *faute de mieux*, the leading lady. The revue was to be called *The Gate Revue*.

Everyone worked terrifically hard to make the revue slick, sophisticated, and fast-moving. Diana Morgan and her husband Robert MacDermot wrote a lot of the show, but we also got some brilliant material from Gerrard Bryant, Ronnie Hill, and dear Arthur Marshall.

We opened the revue with Wally Crisham dressed up as the Lord Chamberlain, complete with coronet and robes and standing behind a silver gate as we sang:

> *Oh please Mr Censor open the gate?*
> *No, Sir, No Sir,*
> *Three bags full of taboos*

By today's standards, the revue was immaculately clean, but I suppose some sketches were then considered a little risqué. One called "Hairdressers Confessions" was about women who confide their inmost secrets to their hairdressers, who assume a priest-like role; another sketch was about male dress designers who create such hideously outlandish fashions that women end up looking so ridiculous that men aren't attracted to them. The sketch ended:

> *For you see, dear Jane and Mary*
> *Dame fashion is a fairy*
> *And the fairies will get you if you don't watch out.*

I was lucky to be given some marvellous numbers in *The Gate Revue* like "Beauty Beauty"—a send-up of women's fitness campaigns that would still be pretty topical today—and "Spin", a skit on the fairy-tale lady endlessly spinning.

> *Spin,*
> *Spin,*
> *First in out,*
> *Then out in.*

that I wrote with Nicholas Phipps. I was also allowed to perform some other material I'd written myself, including one with me dressed as a spiritualist that began:

> *I'm only a medium medium*
> *My goodness! the men that I've known.*
> *What with giving seances,*
> *And falling in trances,*
> *I don't spend a night on my own.*

67

I wrote another monologue called "Bicycling", where a cycling enthusiast instructs the audience how to make their own bicycles. I had difficulty getting suitable clothes for my bicycling lady. I wanted her to look real and I spent many days exploring second-hand clothes shops as far apart as Shepherds Bush and the Mile End Road until I found what I considered just right. I often found my most successful revue costumes in secondhand shops and markets.

Geoffrey Wright wrote a sentimental showstopping hit song called "Transatlantic Lullaby", which Gabrielle Brune sang, and by the dress rehearsal, we knew the show was going to be a success. The press liked it enormously and I also got rave notices. Then came an invasion by West End managers who wanted to transfer the show but wanted a star instead of me. Norman Marshall, bless him, stood firm and told all the managements that if they wanted the show, they would have to take me as well. He was so insistent that they agreed and we ended up in a small West End theatre—the Ambassadors. I was, and still am, eternally grateful to Norman for standing by me; and I feel any success I've had, I owe to him.

Of course, a transfer to the West End meant the Lord Chamberlain had to approve the script, and we began to regret our bold opening number. Our script came back with a few blue pencil marks, but I think the only item we had to cut completely was the male dress designers sketch. The Lord Chamberlain actually seemed quite sympathetic; he said how much he'd enjoyed reading the show, and his office suggested alternative comedy lines in place of the ones they apologised for cutting!

Of course, the most suggestive number in the *Revue* was "Spin", which was passed without a cut as it looked so innocent—on paper.

The Gate Revue ran for 126 performances at the Ambassadors Theatre and Norman started planning a second edition of the show, which was to be called *Swinging the Gate*. Before rehearsals started, I was allowed to take a holiday.

Eric had promised in the early days of our marriage to take me to America and he kept his word even though we were about to be divorced. We sailed on the *Ile de France* and that Atlantic crossing, the first of so many for me, was the roughest of them all. I lay sick for the entire voyage, while Eric was fine and had a ball with several well-known film stars.

My first impression of New York was strangely unfavourable. It seemed too hectic and too concentrated, or maybe I was still feeling ill from the beastly crossing. Eric had booked us into the Gotham Hotel, where we found a demented woman waiting for us. He introduced her as the person he was going to marry once we were divorced. The woman—perhaps I should be kind and say girl—the woman said she didn't see why Eric should have kept his promise to take me to America and she threatened to kill herself if she had to play second fiddle to me. The situation looked grim as far as I could tell, but Eric said not to worry and he disappeared with her into her bedroom. He was away for an hour (he was a wonderful lover) and he had no more trouble from her . . . till he married her.

Eric took the woman with him to Hollywood, where he'd been engaged to write the screenplay for *Goodbye Mr Chips*. I thought it endearingly diplomatic of me not to accompany them there; in any case, I wanted to stay on and see New York.

Eric rented me a little flat on the East Side on Forty-seventh Street—which was just becoming fashionable—and in case of need, he left some money in the bank for me. Unfortunately, I couldn't remember which one. By now it must be quite a sum. Even now, if I have nothing better to do, I try to find out which bank has the money. I never have liked banks; I like to keep my money where I can count it.

My flat was charming, but Eric had told me that the neighbourhood was not safe and he made me promise not to go out alone. As I didn't know a soul in New York, this was rather limiting and I had to stay in a good deal. Vincent Price was my only visitor and he could only come to see me once as he was en route to

69

Hollywood. I'd met Vincent in London when he'd come over to play Prince Albert in *Victoria Regina* at the Gate Theatre. As the Prince, he had to play "Drink to me only with thine eyes" on the piano, and as he had never played before, I took him up to my flat in the Adelphi to teach him how to sing and play. He proved to be a very able pupil.

In New York, apart from Vincent, I only saw the daily lady who came in to clean the flat. She arrived in her own car, very different from my woman in London. I was so impressed by her means of transport that I always got up early and tidied up the flat and washed the dishes before she arrived.

I was so terribly lonely on that first visit to New York that I was thankful it was only a short one, and it was a relief to return to London on the *Queen Mary*.

I arrived safely in London, and everything was as I'd left it. The maid, the cat, masses of letters greeted me, and the war rumours had temporarily died down. I unpacked and decided to have a bath. While I was soaking, my maid poked her head round the door and said, "There's a very tall, good-looking young man at the door who says he's your son." Her voice reflected disbelief.

"He probably is," I said. "Put him in the sitting room and tell him I'll be out in a minute." I jumped out of my bath, put on a bathrobe, combed my hair, and went to meet my son Stephen whom I hadn't seen since he was a baby.

We talked about the past, the present, and the future. We were, after all the years of separation, still mother and son, and more importantly, we liked each other. He told me he hadn't been allowed to mention my name at home and he didn't know whether I would welcome him coming to see me without warning.

"How did you find out where I was living?" I enquired.

"The phone book. I didn't think you'd be in it, but you were." Thank God, against the advice of my friends, I had a listed number and address! I hate unlisted phones—they never ring.

We discussed the probability of war and Stephen said if there was a war (which he very much doubted), he was going to enlist in the Navy; but the war seemed, at that moment, so unlikely that it didn't take up much of our conversation. We talked mostly about the theatre. He also told me he was sharing a flat with a girl, and they were making their own furniture; he said proudly, "She makes all her own clothes." It didn't seem too promising to me and I never met her. They parted when war broke out and, as he said he would, he joined the Royal Navy.

The next time I met him was after the war. He was very proud of the medal he'd got for rescuing the ship's dog, who fell overboard in a rough sea. I think he was almost as proud of this as he was of the DSC which he also received—for bravery in action. By then Stephen was reading English at Cambridge University. He was a member of Footlights, the university drama society, and every year they put on a revue. I went down to see it and was a little taken aback to find that it contained an impersonation of me! Nevertheless, it was a very good show. I'd missed so many of Stephen's birthdays that I decided for once to give him a really good present. So I hired a West End theatre and brought the whole Footlights company to London to give one special performance. Since then, *The Footlights Revue* has come to London regularly, but it was my venture that started it off.

Stephen later became a lecturer at Manchester University, where he was the first ever British fellow of Drama. He went on to direct a theatre company at Stoke-on-Trent and eventually took a house at Scarborough in Yorkshire and started a theatre-in-the-round in the old town library. He tried to encourage new young writers and one of the playwrights he discovered and presented there was Alan Ayckbourn. Stephen died of cancer in 1967 and

Alan Ayckbourn now lives in his old house and still premieres all his plays in Stephen's theatre, which he has renamed The Stephen Joseph Memorial Theatre.

With the second faint whispers of war, my mother fled to Cornwall. Most people felt sure that if war was declared, London was bound to be bombed. Countless people started to leave the capital. My mother never said good-bye to any of us, not even her sisters; she just vanished to Cornwall and booked herself into a nursing home, as all the hotels were full. I waited to see what Mr Chamberlain had up his sleeve, but I hadn't much faith there was anything up there but his arm.

The BBC evacuated their classical orchestra to Wales, and I was a guest at the first concert they gave there. What part I took in the concert, I don't remember. Anyway, I was called to the phone during rehearsal to speak to the matron of my mother's nursing home in Cornwall. She told me that my mother had jumped out of a second-floor window and killed herself. She said there was to be an inquest and asked me whether I would come and sort things out.

After the concert, I got in a train and left Wales for Cornwall and the coroner's court. My mother had left a letter that the coroner said I'd better not read, but I felt that I should. She gave a reason for her suicide—the bad treatment she had from her sisters, and she listed them by name. Contrary to what she wrote, the aunts had all shown her great kindness and patience and all had asked her to stay with them when my father died. Her letter was so unjust and full of hate that I started to cry. The coroner said, "I told you not to read it; give it back to me," which I did.

"Now there's no need for you to stay any longer," he said kindly. I made the necessary arrangements and returned to London.

O n September 3rd, 1939, at 11 AM, Neville Chamberlain spoke on the radio to inform us that our ultimatum to the Germans to withdraw their troops from Poland had not been answered and consequently we were now at war with Germany.

This came as no surprise to anybody and obediently we all toddled off to the local town hall to get our gas masks. We were told these were essential and were led to believe that the Germans would immediately start dropping gas bombs with the idea of choking off the civilian population or at least cowering them. The Germans didn't drop their gas bombs, but we all slung our obligatory gas masks over our shoulders and carried them with us wherever we went. We weren't allowed in restaurants or theatres without them, but I'm afraid I was always absentmindedly leaving mine behind me in shops or restaurants, so I was constantly at the town hall queuing up for a new one. After my fifth appearance, they refused to give me another, so I bought a gas mask case, stuffed it with paper, and got away with it. What I would have done if the Germans had dropped gas bombs, I don't know—but I baulked at the silliness of having a hideous memento slung over my shoulder. I say *silliness* because I'm sure the damn things were useless, though I must say I'm glad I never had to prove it.

There was quite a long gap before the Germans started bombing London with real bombs. This phoney war ended in May 1940, with the German invasion of France and the lowland countries; and with the evacuation of the British Army from Dunkirk, it was felt that Germany would invade England next. We were desperately short of guns and the weapons of modern warfare. To compensate, elderly gentlemen raided theatrical costumiers and there was a run on scimitars, pikes, blunderbusses, bows and arrows, swords and foils—anything that they could use to defend their homes.

During their invasion of Europe, the Germans had dropped paratroopers disguised as nuns into Holland. Now rumours were rife that parachutists disguised as nuns might land in England. Official guidelines were issued, warning us to be suspicious of any nuns with machine guns under their habits and informing us that the way to tell German nuns from real ones was by their feet, as the false nuns wore big boots and had very big feet. It was a bad time for nuns.

Old ladies who lived in the country near Portsmouth and spotted solitary men or nuns in their gardens would pretend to be friendly and offer them tea and poisoned sandwiches, convinced they were German paratroopers on their way to blow up Portsmouth Harbour. I know it all sounds mad but it's quite true. The government peppered Portsmouth and London, and I presume the entire country, with posters telling us not to indulge in careless talk. You couldn't say, "I shall miss you but I think you're very wise to move to Richmond" over the phone to your grandfather without laying yourself open to being rebuked and cut off.

Meanwhile, I was back at the Gate Theatre rehearsing *Swinging the Gate*. The revue showed as much bite and promise as its predecessor had. *Swinging the Gate* had the same format as *The Gate Revue*, but the material was completely new and this time was centred around me by design, not accident.

Eric and Jack Strachey wrote me a very funny spoof operatic number "Queen of Song": "Queen of song. I'm the reason that tenors go wrong". But my favourite was "I Spy", which I wrote with Jack about the headmistress of a school for spies.

The reviews for *Swinging the Gate* were as ecstatic as they had been before and again we transferred to the Ambassadors Theatre. The cast for the West End included Bobby Helpmann, who didn't dance a step but was quite wonderful doing impersonations, and Peter Ustinov, whom I'd seen doing an act at the Players' Club in Covent Garden. I was enchanted by him and insisted on his being in the revue. We gave him two spots that were supposed to last a maximum of three minutes each, but Peter ended up making each last for ten. "Consternation Piece", which he wrote himself, was extremely fresh and funny.

In the opening scene when we were all sitting on the grass having a picnic, Peter (for reasons I've never found out) was wearing his other two changes under his white flannel suit —which gave him a strange appearance. He started the evening rather fat and as the show progressed, he got slimmer by degrees. Perhaps he hoped people would notice and put it down to the energy he expended giving his all. Of course, he was a huge success in the show, and I can't think why he hardly speaks to me nowadays when we meet.

The cast of *Swinging the Gate* also included a young Ronald Millar, who went on to achieve great success as a playwright. He numbers *Abelard and Héloïse*, *Robert and Elizabeth*, and speeches for Prime Minister Margaret Thatcher among his greatest hits. I liked Ronnie enormously and from time to time we still commit an act of telephony.

As the war hotted up, bombs began to fall on London thick and fast, and most of the West End theatres closed. I think only two remained open—the Ambassadors, where we were playing, and the Windmill, where they had nude shows. The censor had decided nudity was permissible as long as the nudes didn't move, but "if it moves, it's rude", said the Lord Chamberlain. Then the German raids intensified and after a particularly bad Saturday-night raid, there were several large bomb craters on main roads in the West End. These so disorganised the traffic that the audience couldn't get to the theatres even if they'd wanted to. On Monday morning, the cast and management met on the stage of the Ambassadors Theatre and reluctantly agreed it was impossible to carry on—and even *Swinging the Gate* came to an abrupt close.

I'll never forget that Monday morning; I was heartbroken. Fate seemed so cruel, for just as I was gaining success, everything seemed to fall apart. But I couldn't feel sorry for myself for long. So many people were losing their homes, their sweethearts, and their lives that it would have been petty for me to feel bitter.

I was terrified by the bombing, and with all London's theatres closed, it seemed pointless to stay in the city. So I gave up my former blacksmith's forge and sent my furniture to the country, where Brian Desmond Hurst, the film director, gave it a home in his barn.

I intended to leave London myself; but before leaving, my divorce from Eric was finalised. As I was divorcing him, I had to attend court. I've always found it impossible to remember dates, and my mind went blank when the judge started asking me when Eric and I had met, when we'd been married, how long the marriage had lasted, and how long we'd been separated. I couldn't answer any of his questions and my lawyer started trying to help me by holding up his fingers. I tried to peer across at him and he appeared to be holding up five fingers.

"Five years," I told the judge confidently. My lawyer started waving his arms wildly and held up three fingers. "Sorry, three years," I said firmly.

I studied my lawyer's latest semaphore signal. "Ah, thirty-five years—no, I mean nineteen thirty-five." By now my lawyer was looking very like a tic tac man at the races and I began to laugh. The sober judge followed my eyeline and his august eyes rested on my gesticulating lawyer. Fortunately the judge saw the funny side too and granted me my freedom. It was a crazy divorce.

I then took my cat and my maid and moved to the country to stay with Brian Desmond Hurst. Brian's country home was called "Wardrobes Lodge". It was very old and most beautiful, situated in the heart of the Buckinghamshire countryside, amid acres of forests and fields—with no houses for miles around.

Dear Brian was the nicest, sweetest, most wicked man I've ever known. He was also an excellent film director and much ahead of his time. *Dangerous Moonlight* was probably his best-known film success. Brian always had some handsome young man staying with him.

When I arrived at "Wardrobes", I met a young Battle of Britain Air Force pilot there named Victor. One night, very late, he came into the house and woke me up, saying, "Brian says he's sick of me and if you don't let me sleep with you—and Brian said you would—I'll kill myself."

Victor was all of nineteen and was as wild as he could be without being put away. I didn't know how to get rid of him and as I was half asleep, I didn't bother. He became my lover for a long time. Brian disapproved but as he'd started it, he had to put up with the consequences. Victor used to spend all his leaves at

"Wardrobes" and for a time, he was stationed quite near. He used to frighten us all to death by flying his plane low over the house, waving and shouting.

"Wardrobes" was far enough from London for us to feel comparatively safe and yet if we climbed a nearby hill, it was possible to see London far in the distance. I remember lying on the grass with Victor one night and in the hush of the summer night watching the Blitz over London—once only, for it was horrible to lie in the stillness and watch the shells bursting like golden rain and the quivering red glow in the sky, and to be caught, even for a moment, by the beauty of it, knowing what hell had broken loose over the city.

While I was living at "Wardrobes", Brian had a meeting of film moguls. They came to tea to discuss what was to happen to the British film industry during the war, and I was the hostess. When we ran short of milk, Brian rang for the local country boy who was temporarily employed as general factotum before being called up for the Navy.

"Can we have some more milk?" asked Brian.

"Sure, Mr Hurst, I'll just go and tweak the cow's tit."

That loosened us all up and the party was a great success; the important purpose of the meeting was quite forgotten.

I was longing to get back to work, but no offers came and I was beginning to wonder whether I should have the guts to go back to London. Staying at Brian's was enormous fun. He usually had an interesting selection of houseguests. Hector Bolitho, Anton Walbrook, and Rodney Ackland, the playwright, often came to stay; and William Golding came to leave some precious books and pictures in safety while he went to America to do a lecture tour. These guests came for a few days' rest and then left—I stayed on. I didn't want to outstay my welcome and just as I was wondering what I should do, out of a clear blue sky—which by the way is a misnomer as the clear blue sky was full of barrage balloons—an offer came for me to co-star with Hermione Baddeley in a revue called *Rise Above It*.

I returned to London to find a new place to live. It wasn't hard to find accommodation as so many people had left the city. In fact, just as I was returning, anyone with any sense was leaving. I found a charming little house to rent in Kinnerton Street, Belgravia, which was very nicely furnished and cheap, so I moved in leaving the maid and cat at "Wardrobes" with Brian. It wasn't until I slept my first night in Kinnerton Street that I realised how near it was to the anti-aircraft guns in Hyde Park; and when the guns came into action, the house jumped and rocked in the air. If by any rare chance I had to spend a night alone (particularly if it was a fine moonlight night—clear for the bombers), I didn't undress but just lay down on the bed dressed in trousers and a sweater and with a torch at hand. If I slept for one hour, I was lucky, but mostly I lay awake listening to the shrapnel falling on the roof.

Rise Above It was a jolly good show and we had a long run at the Comedy Theatre. Hermione Baddeley and I weren't overly fond of each other. I found her very unprofessional; she'd alter lines and business without warning, which made it impossible to play a sketch to get the maximum effect and balance. She'd upstage, tread on laughs, and insert unfunny gags designed to amuse the cast more than the audience. Often in the middle of a sketch, she'd hiss under her breath, "What's my next line?" Well, I had enough trouble remembering my own lines; why should I re-member hers, too? There was tension between us from the start, for before our contracts were signed, we had to establish which of us was to have top billing. Naturally, we were both reluctant to be on the right side of the posters, and the show was in jeopardy of being cancelled until our producer, Jack de Leon, came up with the idea of two sets of bills and placards to be used on alternate weeks.

We encountered the same problem some years later when we co-starred in *Fallen Angels*. The solution that time was for Angus McBean to take some very clever photographs of us that were capable of being used either way up—with me at the top-right corner and Baddeley upside down on the bottom left, or vice versa. The photograph became quite celebrated and even now is often cited as "early inventive photography". Although it does make my blood boil if I chance to come across it displayed the wrong way up.

I liked Angus McBean's portraits so much that I later got him to take my passport photo. Unfortunately, I photograph extremely badly. My pale blue eyes are my best feature and they never show in black-and-white photos. If I want a good photograph, I have to be very carefully lit, preferably by candles, and taken from a distance of twelve miles.

The passport photo Angus McBean took was good enough to get me through Ellis Island, although he rather blotted his copy-book during our photographic session by calling me Miss Baddeley. He looked so covered in confusion that I refrained from referring to his *faux pas* but I felt obliged to redress the balance by calling him Mr Beaton for the remainder of the sitting.

Considering Hermione Baddeley and I only appeared in three shows together, it's strange our names have so often been linked. I suppose it's because there is a great similarity in our Christian names. Just to make matters more confusing, Baddeley's nickname is Totie and mine is Toni. I've never understood it, but I have been told the clash of our personalities on stage created some sort of special magic. Nothing more than sheer hatred spilling across the footlights.

It always makes me mad when I hear myself referred to as "one of the two Hermiones". If ever I'm referred to as that, I usually put the offender in his or her place by asking, "Is there another Hermione?"

The director, or should I say referee, of *Rise Above It* was Henry Kendall; and Wilfrid Hyde-White was particularly funny playing a soldier who on returning from the front came to see the show and didn't know what it was all about.

My favourite sketch was "Hats" written by Denis Waldock. In it, Baddeley and I played two self-centred old dowagers trying on a variety of hideous hats in a millinery shop as we kept up a banter of silly gossip about ourselves and the war.

"If this war goes on much longer, we shall all be living on grass."

"But I don't like grass."

"It will grow on you."

One of the hits of the show was a monologue I wrote myself. It was a pompous pseudo-intellectual "talk on music" which I pronounced mewsick. The subject of my talk was Bucalossi's "Grasshopper's Dance": "And does it remind you just a little of Mozart? No, it does not." Many people thought I had invented Bucalossi and his grasshopper's dance, but he and his dance were absolutely genuine. In fact, years later when I was in London doing *A Little Night Music,* his son turned up at the stage door and said how much his father had enjoyed my music talk.

I also had a divine song—called "I like a little bit of ballet with my lunch"—about a culture vulture who would rather forgo her three-course lunch to spend her one and sixpence on feeding her spirit with poetry in motion. Her plea was:

> *Just a piece of cake that's seedy,*
> *and a faun that's après midi*

It was a charming number and had a touch of pathos without being coy or twee.

Both Baddeley and I got good reviews for *Rise Above It,* but Herbert Farjeon went rather overboard for me, writing: "What a wit, what a witherer, what a human draught Miss Gingold is. Her lampoons are like beating old carpets, making the dust fly up to the cobwebs in the rafters."

All the cast of *Rise Above It* kept hamsters; we started with four and ended up with twenty-four. They roamed from dressing room to dressing room, eating the makeup and generally misbehaving. The management said they must go, so we kept them —but roaming was taboo.

A rat who appeared at one matinée created quite a scene. He or

81

she came up from the bowels of the orchestra pit, walked around the orchestra pit rail, looked at the show for a few minutes, and then made a slow exit. Meanwhile, our woman pianist, a Miss Hero de Rance, turned out to be no hero—for glancing up from her piano, she found herself eye to eye with the rat, gave a piercing scream, and tried to climb out of the orchestra pit. She got one leg over the rail but her remaining leg wouldn't follow, whereupon she fainted clean away. The audience thought it was all part of the show and the box office told me that people rang up and before buying tickets, asked whether the rat would be appearing.

The raids were becoming more frequent and the bombs bigger, and Hermione Baddeley and I often spent the night at Rosa Lewis's famous hotel, the Cavendish, which was very near the theatre. Rosa Lewis was all I had heard about her, so I wasn't surprised when she asked us, "Which of you girls would like to sleep with the Duke of Coverley?" When we replied that neither of us would, she said, "If you'd like some champagne, just ask for it and I'll put it on Lord so-and-so's account."

Last time I was in London, I went to look for the Cavendish Hotel, but it had gone and in its place a big new Cavendish Hotel reared its modern head. Time marches on, I told myself.

In *Sky High* at the Phoenix Theatre, Hermione Baddeley and I were co-starring again. Also in the cast were Elizabeth Welch and wicked Wally Crisham. Before the first rehearsal, Wally rushed over to me in a restaurant, saying, "Super to see you darling. What a lovely blouse you're wearing—and such a long red tie."

I said, "This is no tie—I've just heard you're going to be in the show and I've cut my throat." That was the sort of quip Wally appreciated.

Before *Sky High* opened in London, we went on a short provincial tour. Totie, Wally and I used to try and stay at the same hotel. I must say we had fun.

One night in Nottingham, we were walking around trying to find somewhere to get a meal after the show. The only place open seemed to be a rather unprepossessing café, but we went in, sat down, and ordered fish and chips. Inevitably, we started discussing the show. Then one of the local inhabitants eyed us up, swayed over to our table, and asked, "You're from the theatre, aren't you?" We nodded. A fatal mistake, for he dragged a chair over to our table and sat down.

"I've seen the posters for your show. Are you two sisters?" he asked Totie and me.

In my efforts to explain that because we share the same Christian name, it didn't necessarily follow that we were in any way related, I heard myself saying, "I am Hermione Baddeley and that"—pointing to Totie—"is Hermione Gingold." Totie giggled and said sleepily, "How silly I am, I thought it was the other way round!"

Fascinated by our inability to untangle ourselves, our uninvited guest continued. "I like talking to theatricals—I'm not hidebound. No, I'm a Bohemian myself. I've been about—I haven't lived in Nottingham all my life."

"You've travelled?" asked Wally.

"Oh, yes—Leeds, Hull, Birmingham, I've seen them all." He scanned our faces and we overacted like mad. I showed astonishment; Totie, envy; and Wally, incredulity. I found his faith that we should be impressed rather touching and even Wally—instead of murmuring one of his usual wisecracks—said, "Yes, you must have seen life."

The stranger fixed Totie with a condescending smile and said, "I suppose you theatre people see a bit of the country. What's the nicest place you've visited?" I waited with horror for Totie to tell of her journeys to the South of France, Canada, Greece, or Czechoslovakia.

"I like Blackpool," she said firmly.

"I've never been there," he confessed. "I hear it's very jolly."

I thought of Blackpool, which we'd played the week before. "Yes, very jolly," I said.

"So's Southend," said Wally, determined not to be outdone.

"So's Grimsby," said Totie, going a hundred times too far.

"That's strange," said our friend. "I've been there and I've never found it so."

"You have to know the ropes," said Totie with a knowing leer, and went into a long description of nightlife in the Plaka district of Athens, transferring it with consummate skill into Grimsby. I felt she was going a little over the top, though, when she said, "When the bouzuki music starts, all the men link arms and dance, and then the good people of Grimsby smash every plate in the place."

I saw a suspicious look come into our friend's eye, so we finished our ginger beer quickly, bade him farewell, and made our exit.

If one has the right companions, such commonplace occurrences can make even the dullest tours fun. As we walked back to our hotel, Wally asked whether we couldn't turn our café encounter into a revue sketch. "No, dear," Totie and I agreed. "Too farfetched."

The reviews for *Sky High* weren't as good as the ones we'd got for *Rise Above It*; in fact, they were quite disappointing. Then the press got to hear that there was no love lost between Totie and me, and they built our relationship up into an almighty feud. They exaggerated madly and went so far as to say that we weren't on speaking terms, which wasn't true at all. We spoke to each other onstage every evening.

Of course, our so-called rivalry was wonderful for business and when we were asked to write articles about each other, we did so, and we both thought the articles were very funny.

Baddeley began hers by saying she had no words to adequately appraise my rich qualities—no words fit to appear in print. She went on to say that she was one of my greatest admirers because what was good enough for her grandmother was good enough for her! She claimed she chastised carping critics who'd laid odds that I'd never make the grade.

"Where are those critics now," she asked, "and what good have their winnings done them?" She ended by hoping that "one day she'll find her real niche in life and get what she deserves."

I began my article by saying, "It is not generally known, I think, that Hermione Baddeley is my mother." I continued pretending she was my mother and I was forced to confess she had not been a good mother to me—and the fact that she was years younger than I was no excuse. I praised my mother's war record, especially her achievements in the Crimea and in the reliefs of Lord and Lady Smith, and I admitted, "I think I can truthfully say she never spared herself or the troops in her efforts to entertain them."

Explaining I was working hard because I was busy saving for my mother's old age—due next week—and fearing she was coming to depend on me too much, I concluded by proclaiming that we had discovered blood to be thicker than water.

Sky High ran for seven months, but I'd like to skip *Sky High* and get on to *Sweet and Low*, which started me on my way to real stardom. It was my show and depended on me for a successful run. The *Sweet and Low* revues ran all through the rest of the war

85

and created a long-run record, beaten only by *Chu-Chin-Chow*. Not bad for a satirical revue that was difficult to put on with most able-bodied men called up and all clothes and shoes rationed. The government had said on the one hand that they wanted theatres to stay open whenever possible; on the other, they'd made it practically impossible for them to do so.

Sweet and Low became *Sweeter and Lower* and its final edition was called *Sweetest and Lowest*. The critics were wonderful to me. They called me "Queen Wasp" and "Malice in Wonderland" and described me as a blend of "scorpion, wasp, and poison ivy" —well, I never was the sweet lovable type. J. C. Trewin said that I could "survey the scene with the air of a medieval commander about to spend some brisk hours with his captives and a fresh thumbscrew." This lovely venom was probably inspired by a number called "Borgia Orgy" by John Jowett, where, pretending to be Margaret Lockwood pretending to be Lucretia Borgia, I sang:

> *The Borgias are having an orgy,*
> *There's a Borgia orgy tonight.*
> *But isn't it sickening—*
> *We've run out of strychnine:*
> *The gravy will have to have ground glass for thickening.*
> *When the butler flings open the dining room door*
> *There's a cunning contraption concealed in the floor.*
> *We wonder who'll sit on the circular saw?*
> *At the Borgia orgy tonight.*

Charles Hickman directed all three editions, and Walter Crisham was my leading man for the first year. When he left to tour the Middle East, Henry Kendall took his place. I felt entertaining the troops in England was just as important as entertaining them abroad, and if we'd both left, the show would have closed.

I always got on well with Henry Kendall, except once. We were on stage when, for no reason and with no warning, he tried to "improve" a sketch we had been doing together successfully for two months. I didn't speak to him for three days. That did the trick and from then on, we altered or updated material only after prior discussion.

A young Air Force officer named Alan Melville wrote a lot of material for the first edition, including a number where I moaned:

> *I do Miss Hermione Badly—*
> *I sit in my room just before we begin*
> *and imagine her back again drinking my gin.*

I mopped my eyes with a white handkerchief that had a black border around it. Alan Melville went on to write pretty well all the second and third editions of the show, and I believe he wrote some of his best material lying on a camp bed in an RAF tent pitched by a swamp in Normandy. Sometimes we gave him suggestions about the sort of numbers we wanted and at other times he came up with extraordinary and unexpected sketches like "Picasso" which was a send-up of modern art and in which I played an unhappy multi-coloured female lumbered with two extra limbs and with an outsize fishbone impaled on my head.

I think Alan originally wrote "Young Woodley's Son" for Wally Crisham, but I liked it so much that I did it myself, dressed as an evil little boy in an Eton suit.

"The Cellist" by Leslie Julian Jones was also written for Wally, but as soon as I read it, I knew it was for me. I found a bowlegged bluestocking lady cellist who waddles across the stage moaning "If I'd only never taken up the cello, I wouldn't have to walk like this today" irresistible. The punch line of the monologue was "I wish I'd never taken up the bloody thing". The Lord Chamberlain jumped on the "bloody" like a ton of bricks, but he finally agreed I could say it as long as I didn't make it sound like a swear word. The "Cello" sketch was a great success and apparently it did have a female prototype, as Leslie Julian Jones told me years later that the idea for the monologue was sown when he heard that Sir

Thomas Beecham had once interrupted an orchestral rehearsal to address the lady cellists who were not giving him satisfaction. Sir Thomas tapped his baton impatiently, saying, "Ladies, ladies, you have the most beautiful instrument in the world between your legs and all you can do is scratch it."

Another very successful monologue was "Mother India" which I wrote as a mock-imperialistic talk being delivered by a lady in black velvet and pearls with all the authority of one who has spent two weeks in Delhi:

India is, and has been for some time, the home of the Indians—and that is why it is called India.

In one edition, we had a marvellous finale, where we lowered an enormous song sheet down and got the audience to sing along. It was a familiar tune, but the words rather lampooned the country's then Labour government, which was causing a certain amount of discontent. The audience always sang along eagerly and really belted out the last line—"We've all got labour pains"—before they realised the significance of the words they were singing. It never failed that, as the penny dropped, the entire audience collapsed with laughter and squirmed as if they really did have labour pains.

From the start, our audiences consisted mostly of American and British troops and women in uniform. Jimmy Dolittle, the US general, had a permanent box at the theatre and he gave instructions that any evening he wasn't using it himself, it could be given to American servicemen.

One eccentric young man always bought two seats although he was alone, and in the empty seat next to him, he used to prop up a painting of his grandmother. This naturally annoyed other theatre patrons who, finding all the seats sold, were restricted to standing room only. When they complained and asked him to remove his grandmother's picture, he'd say, "I paid for this seat and she stays."

For the rest of the war, we played all through the raids. At one stage, there were only five London theatres open out of thirty and ours was one of them. Although I was terrified, I tried not to show it. I was the leading lady and had to set an example to the rest of the cast. On matinée days, I always went to work by tube; the nearest station to the theatre was Leicester Square, where the stage manager would meet me and, holding a big umbrella over my head, would walk me to the Ambassadors Theatre. The umbrella was a must, for you never knew what was likely to fall out of the sky. What use the umbrella would have been in a raid, I've since wondered, but at the time it made me feel safe.

In the dark winter evenings, it was quite difficult to get to the theatre. The blackout made it hard to find one's way and torch batteries were in short supply. I remember walking to the theatre one dark night holding a lighted candle in my hand to show me the way.

If there was still a raid in progress when the show finished, the audience had to stay in the theatre until the all clear sounded, which meant we had to go on entertaining them. Sometimes we'd have to stay in the theatre till dawn giving the audiences impromptu concerts or dances. Frequently, other theatres—with straight plays running—would ring up and try to borrow some of our artists to go over and entertain their audiences. If any members of our audiences wanted to come up on to the stage and help us to entertain our captive patrons by doing a "party piece", we were more than delighted. It got to the point when most of the audience arrived with their accompanists, longing for an air raid so they could get up on the stage and do their stuff. I'll never forget a particularly bad raid one night. We might have been seconds from death, but we stood in the wings trying to suppress our laughter as an enthusiastic lady—who was old enough to know better—sang, "Lo! Hear the gentle lark" with bomb obbligato.

After the show at night, everyone in the cast had to take turns going on the roof of the theatre. If a firebomb fell, it had to be picked up and thrown into the street. I was excused this chore, as the management felt I would do more harm than good. On the nights I was supposed to be on the roof, I always stayed in my dressing room to serve hot soup and sandwiches to my stand-in.

Food had become scarce in London—most things were reduced to powder. I learned to make quite good omelettes with powdered eggs. There were hardly any fruit or vegetables; most milk was reserved for invalids and babies, yet we were all healthy without the foods that nowadays are considered essential to our well-being. Where food is concerned, I've never been a dainty nibbler, but throughout the war I devoured everything with a wolflike determination to swallow all I could before a bomb fell. Naturally, this made me a very messy eater. My maid would take my clothes to the cleaners, commenting, "You had a good dinner last night; I see from the front of this dress . . . you started with tomato soup, then fish cakes with mm . . . anchovy sauce, and quite a good trifle to follow."

This inspired me to write a sketch about a woman who practically dined off her clothes.

Chocolate was rationed and I missed it so much that I think I would have committed murder to get it, but the cast, dear souls, gave me their coupons so I could indulge myself, and no one got murdered.

One of the cast who used to pass me her coupons was dear Gretchen Franklin. I'll never forget the time I was going away for the weekend and in my arm I was cradling what looked like a large sheaf of flowers. Gretchen rushed up to me, saying, "What a beautiful bouquet," only to find my bouquet was three heads of celery wrapped in newspaper.

90

The Ivy restaurant was an excellent eating house opposite the theatre which was frequented by theatrical celebrities and famous people. I looked around one night and there were so many stars eating there that I remember thinking, "If a bomb fell here tonight, they wouldn't be able to cast a West End play for months." One night at the Ivy, they had whale steaks on the menu. I thought they were terrible and couldn't eat them. I must admit they looked like steak, but when you cut into them, they were sort of purply and tasted fishy.

The Ivy restaurant was a hotbed of delicious gossip and its clientele, myself included, was expert at dishing out all sorts of dirt on Hitler, Goebbels, and our fellow artists. This led us to do a sketch in the show called "Poison Ivy". Henry Kendall and I were in what was supposed to be the Ivy restaurant, where we sat discussing the West End stars frequenting the venue.

"Look who Errol Flynn's with—that will cause a sensation."

"But Hermione, he's alone."

"That's what I mean."

"Oh look, there's Florence Desmond doing an imitation of John Gielgud. Oh no, it *is* John Gielgud." I also delivered the line that has become a classic: "Laurence Olivier was a tour de force, but Donald Wolfit was forced to tour."

It all sounds pretty tame now when everyone is lampooned mercilessly on television, but in 1942 it was considered novel and daring to name names. We were constantly updating "the dirt" to keep our references topical. Strangely enough, our maligned victims seemed to love being singled out for our whiplash treatment. I think the only person who was really upset was J. B. Priestley, who objected to the lines "Who's that talking to J. B. Priestley?" "Not talking dear—listening."

I think most of the other celebrities were secretly delighted to be mentioned and no one ever sued us. Half the West End stars complained about the wicked things we said and the other half complained they had been ignored.

Ostensibly Alan Melville wrote *Poison Ivy* but in reality I think he just went to the Ivy and wrote down verbatim the worst of the things being said.

I acquired quite a reputation onstage, and off, for being a wit. I described someone as being "as arch as the Admiralty", and when Anna Neagle went off to make yet another of her virtuous heroine films, I told a friend she had gone to star in *A Streetcar Named Respectability*.

One day Alan asked me whether I'd read Tallulah Bankhead's autobiography. "My dear," I told him, "it burst into flames in my hands," and we put my comment into the show.

The critic T. C. Worsley said, "She is indeed the archetypal theatre gossip. . . . To watch Miss Gingold's tongue roll round a familiar name and then quietly drop it off with all the mud sticking on is to watch art raising a foible to the stature of a humour." James Agate described me as "the quintessence of the comic muse", and another paper called me "England's debunker in chief".

A pretentious interviewer once asked me whether I could analyse what he referred to as "my penetratingly satirical sarcasm"; and I suppose I can—bitchy remarks come to me quite naturally.

I know this makes me sound terrible, but I do have some virtues. If I can just have a few days to think of them. Perhaps the best thing you can say about me is that I'm honest, sober, and an early riser.

The audience adored "Poison Ivy", especially the theatrically informed "Gallery First-nighters Club", who appreciated the most subtle theatrical reference. They were a formidable body of theatregoers—a sort of Ku Klux Klan of the theatre world—and it was a triumph that they liked me, for they'd attend a first night en masse and could be very vocal if they didn't like the play. They would yell, "Take it off, it's rubbish" or "We can't hear you, speak up"—generally making their presence known. They were greatly feared by actors, who dreaded them almost more than they did theatre critics.

Sophie Rosen was the ringleader. She went to every first night and was the most vocal of them all. Nevertheless, Sophie used to visit me in my dressing room, bringing Jewish fried fish and other goodies that she must have got on the black market.

On the first night of *Sweetest and Lowest*, I wasn't too worried about the Gallery First-nighters, but I was worried when I heard Noël Coward was in front, for the show included a number lampooning him, which started:

> *In a dressing gown exquisitely flowered*
> *Mr Coward*
> *At the conference which he daily sat on*
> *Advised both Eisenhower and Mountbatten*
> *On the private habits of the lower decks.*

Noël was still firmly in his seat as I finished the number and knowing half the audience was looking at him to see how he'd taken it, he clapped somewhat over-enthusiastically, and I was still apprehensive when I met him at the Ivy after the show.

"Boodles, dear," he said with a touch of frisson, "I should very much like a copy of that little item about me."

"To use for legal proceedings?" I asked.

"No, dear"—he laughed—"to frame."

The Americans made the show, and me, their own and used to flock round the stage door after a performance to thank me for the number I sang called "Thanks Yanks".

Thanks, Yanks! . . .
That very nice boy
From old Illinois
Who led an attack on my flanks—
The least I could say was "thanks".

My favourite Yanks I invited back to Kinnerton Street, and I'm told my little house became known as "Club 81" throughout America.

My GI friends turned up at "Club 81" to use the telephone, have baths, change their clothes, or spend a night on my sitting-room floor when no hotel beds were available.

When I could, I'd try to get out of London on Sundays, going to stay with Brian or my friends the Upsons at Maidenhead—to have a bit of country peace away from Kinnerton Street. I'd leave the GIs in charge of my house and when I returned to London for the Monday show, it was amazing how many complete strangers would stop me in the streets and say, "I went to a wonderful party at your house on Sunday."

I was amazed at the enthusiasm and understanding of the Americans for a show that was full of satire on English happenings, but they loved it—although some of the boys had never been to the theatre before and some hadn't even worn shoes, so they told me. I think they were called hillbillies.

There was one sketch where Henry Kendall dressed up as a duchess who attempted to explain the incongruities of English pantomime to Bonar Colleano as a GI. The American servicemen particularly loved this sketch with its lines such as:

"Say, Duchess, who's the dame?"
"That's not the dame, that's the principal boy."

However, Henry Kendall pretending to be a duchess got some of the audience as confused at the show as Bonar Colleano was supposed to be in the sketch. One strapping US Marine was overheard recommending the show to his friends: "There's this guy who dresses up as a duchess, and there's another guy called Hormone Golding who dresses up as a dame all through the show."

Another aside was overheard by the entire theatre. A misguided woman took a child to a matinée; during a silent pause, the child pointed to me and yelled very audibly, "Mama—what's that woman for?" There's really no answer to that.

I should love to own my own theatre one day, but if ever I do, I should make very firm rules. Children under seven, even if accompanied by one or both parents, will not be sold seats for performances of Ibsen, Chekhov, Euripides, Pinter, or revue —except on public holidays. Also, the audience will not be permitted to eat during a performance and furthermore, people who cough will be given medical attention on the spot. When people try to buy seats at my theatre, they will be asked certain questions, the first being why they want to see the show. People answering, "to get out of the rain" will not be admitted, nor will people who think Shakespeare wrote *Sweeney Todd* or that *The Wild Duck* is a musical.

Sadly, the chances of my owning a theatre in the immediate future are pretty slim. This is a great relief to my business manager, especially when he reads that if I'd owned a theatre in the war, all GIs would have been admitted regardless and gratis, too.

During the war I received some marvellous fan letters from the American GIs. One was addressed to "Herman Gielgud, Ambassadors Theatre, London." The letter was short and to the point: "Dear Sir or Madam, Please could you send me a signed photo." I did so and back came a letter in return that said, "Dear Sir, thank you for the signed photograph." The GIs not only wrote fan letters but they also brought goodies it was impossible for civilians to obtain. I often wondered what their mothers must have thought of their sons' frenzied letters begging them to send false eyelashes, scent, lipstick, brassières, and nylon stockings. Of course, they brought food as well—butter, eggs, and meat came from the PX.

95

They even managed to obtain paint and painted my little house battleship grey. I'll never forget how indignant my neighbours were when a lorry of sailors showed up and proceeded to paint it for me. They hadn't been able to get their own houses painted since before the war began.

All through the run of *Sweet and Low*, I had the same faithful dresser, Kitty Churchill. She'd been a theatrical dresser for years and could remember the time when the Gaiety Girls used to receive magnificent gifts from the stage-door johnnies. She used to say, "In them days, my young ladies used to get orchids, champagne, and precious jewels. How times have changed; now it's half a pound of butter and two eggs."

Victor had gone out of my life. He had been arrested in my dressing room for being AWOL. I begged the officer who came to pick him up to see the show before he took Victor away—which he did; he enjoyed it enormously and said, "I'll see he isn't court-martialled." In a way, I was glad to see Victor go, as he was behaving so badly. I remember going downstairs one day, and at the bottom of the stairs he was standing pointing a revolver at me.

"I'm going to kill you," he shouted.

"But I've got a matinée today."

This must have been a good reason for letting me live, because he apologised and I went off to the theatre—but not before I popped next door and told my friend Chris Hewett what had happened. Chris was also in the revue with me and he went to my house, took Victor's revolver away from him, and put it under the floorboard in his own flat, where I suppose it remains to this day.

Chris Hewett lives in the United States now, where he has had great success as a director and as an actor—particularly in Mel Brooks' film *The Producers*.

I hated being alone, so, unlike many people, I was delighted when I had a charming American billeted with me for a short time. He was with the USO, and I remember one night during a lull in a very bad raid I said to him, "Jimmy, let's go to the Hyde Park tube station shelter."

He said, "Darling, you go. American soldiers aren't allowed to use English civilian shelters." I made him put on my mink and one of my crazy hats and together we raced to the comparative safety of the station and arrived just before the second strafing.

Here I would like to tell you what life was like in the tube stations. They were closed at night, but the public stormed them and the government had to open them up. They became home to many people who, with their families, slept and lived in them during the war. They had their own bunks, some decorated with lace curtains and photos. Some even cooked down there and only came up for a few hours every day to get some fresh air. It really made me feel very sad seeing the babies crawling on the not-so-clean platforms.

Some stations were not used very much as air raid shelters, but the Piccadilly line, which was the deepest underground, always had its stations crowded from dusk to dawn. The nearest station to my house was Hyde Park. It was quite a chic shelter—no bunks, no lace curtains; and unless there was a very bad raid, very few people used it. They took thermos flasks of coffee, champagne, and gramophones with them, and there was dancing on the platforms. Almost a party atmosphere, but the safety of these stations was relative, because if the upstairs station was hit by a bomb, people drowned from bursting water pipes.

I hardly ever used the station, and at night I was picked up from the theatre by Mr Jenkins, who drove his taxi all through the bombing. He was a darling old snob who only drove celebrities.

Mr Jenkins was a marvellous source of gossip. Intimate revue was regarded as being too sophisticated to play the provinces, with the exception of some hotbeds of culture such as Brighton and Cambridge. If we did take the show out on a pre-London tour, I always tried to race back to London on the last train after the show on Saturday night so I could spend Sunday at home. I'd send Mr Jenkins a telegram asking him to pick me up at the station and he never let me down. I'd settle back in his cab and as we drove off into the darkness, Mr Jenkins would—during the twenty-minute drive from the station to Kinnerton Street— make me *au fait* with all the news of first nights: forthcoming theatrical and film productions with their casts and producers; who had given parties and which had been most successful; who was on leave or had been whisked away; who had backed winners, had lost at cards, become engaged, divorced, got born or died.

On our journeys home from the theatre, if the raids were very bad, Mr Jenkins would sometimes stop at the Ritz and we'd go down to its bar, which stayed open all night, acting as the shelter for those staying in the hotel because it was underground. It was fun watching the few residents go down in all sorts of clothing, and some Eastern potentates arriving with their entourages —carrying their jewel cases and fur coats.

When the all clear sounded, we went up to the street again, which was empty except for dustcarts picking up bits and pieces of people from the rubble and putting them in canvas bags.

It was the most immoral time in my life. If I felt I needed an excuse, I had the one of not knowing which day or night was going to be my last. So the loan of my body to a handsome young American who was going to France, who had no one in this strange country to tell his fears to or make love to for what might be the last time, seemed the least I could offer. In a way, I felt it was my contribution to the war effort. I'm not saying I didn't need them as much as they needed me—I did. The days I could cope with; the nights, I had to have company and Jimmy Morcome, my billeted chum, had left me to go to camp.

After the war, when I settled in America, the United Nations honoured me by presenting me with a special medal "For furthering Anglo-American relations". I think a little bird must have told them, possibly a vulture.

I remember B.J. He had been an artist and was worried because he'd lost his feeling for art.

"Well," I said, "I'm writing a book and I'd love it if you would do the illustrations."

"That'd be wonderful," he said, "it'll give me some hope for the future." So I had to start writing a book.

The World Is Square was intended to be a tale of the progress of civilisation from the good old days when a family thought of sitting down to a nice little roast ox for supper up to wartime when such a tasty morsel was all too sadly replaced by a genteel dish of Spam. The plot didn't quite work out as I'd planned it, and it turned into a spoof autobiography where I inhabited a fantasy world of spies and theatre, and my father lived submerged in the lake in Regents Park.

I told some very tall stories in my book.

"Mr Rudyard Kipling was a constant visitor to my grandmother's house in London. He not only read her some of his splendid poems but he also gave her a very jolly Indian scarf, with which she afterwards hung herself." Of course no one was supposed to take this story seriously, but it's amazing how many people came up to me and asked whether they could see the scarf.

I also claimed I was so expert a spy that I could tap out the entire balcony scene from *Romeo and Juliet* in Morse code. "I practised field cooking in the secrecy of my bedroom, and I worked so hard on my camouflage technique that soon I got to the stage where I could reach the bathroom in broad daylight unseen by any member of my family. In fact, my sister once got into the bath while I was still in it, so cleverly was I camouflaged as a sponge."

I sent B.J. pages to illustrate while he was away at a service camp. The most extraordinary thing was that the book got published—which in wartime was a triumph, as very few books were published because of the paper shortage. Though I say so myself, it was a very good book and so were his illustrations. Then the White Knight went off to the front. (I called B.J. the White Knight because he was gentle and sweet, like the White Knight in *Alice Through the Looking Glass*.)

I was so frightened in the war, I hated it so much, and yet I loved it, too. It seems a terrible thing to say, but looking back on it, I think of it as a happy time. Yes, if I'm honest, I enjoyed the war.

Some things stand out in my memory of wartime London with great clarity. The strangeness of living in the city where there were no children, hardly any women except those in uniform, and few animals. The great friendliness of the few people who were left. The night the Germans bombed the docks and you could read the newspaper in the street by the light of the fires. A taxi blown up into a tree in Leicester Square after a bombing of the West End. The night Mr Jenkins arrived late at the theatre, saying Beatrice Lillie had been badly shaken by a "near hit" and he'd had to put her to bed. I have happy memories too of The Stage Door Canteen; it was formerly a coffee shop called The Popular Café, but it was revamped as a makeshift theatre and club for servicemen. I was in the official opening show and, with a rota of other celebrities, often entertained there.

I also vividly remember the afternoon the Queen Mother, the Queen as she was then, broadcast to the women of France when it looked as if France would give up fighting. The theatre staff, stagehands, and all the cast went down to the property room under the Ambassadors stage to hear the broadcast, which was wonderful and sad. The Queen had a perfect accent and yet you could tell it was not a French woman. Somehow she sounded girlish and very British as she begged the French to fight on and promised we would never let them down. You could have heard a pin drop during her speech. Even our tough property men and head electrician had tears in their eyes and so did I.

Sometimes, on Sundays, we took *Sweet and Low* on the road to entertain the troops as part of the war effort. On one occasion, we took it to General Patton's headquarters, which was only an hour from London along the River Thames. My guess is that it was Henley.

While the show was being set up, General Patton asked me whether I'd like to play croquet with him, and I said I'd love to. We went to the lawn that led down to the river and I said, "I suppose you'll push me in if I win." He promised not to, but I noticed he was wearing a mother-of-pearl-handled pistol, so I decided not to draw attention to the fact that he cheated just a little. Our show for him and his staff was a great success and afterwards General Patton drove me back to London in a very luxurious limousine. He amazed me by reciting one of my favourite poems, "Jabberwocky", and that was the last I saw of him, much to my sorrow.

101

I loved being Queen Wasp of London, but I still cherished an unfulfilled ambition to play principal boy in a Christmas panto-mime. Emile Littler was one of the leading impresarios of the day, and I confided my ambition to him. Unfortunately, he thwarted my hopes by telling me I'd be quite unsuitable and far too sophisticated to inflict on the impressionable young minds that attend such shows. Emile said I'd play principal boy with my tongue in my cheek. "On the contrary," I told him, "I take my pantomime seriously." The ultimate put-down came when Emile suggested I'd be more suited to playing the dame.

I was sad as I could see I was becoming stereotyped, but I cheered up when Emile said that to show there were no hard feelings, he was going to send me a "pair of something". I knew Emile was very rich and felt sure I should soon receive a pair of earrings—diamond at least. Some of my cruder friends suggested he might be sending me an item of clothing. In a peak of excitement, we all assembled at The Ambassadors Theatre, as Emile had said my gift would be delivered there at lunchtime the following day.

When two large London taxicabs drew up, I realised my "pair" was too large to be earrings, but I did laugh as the drivers levered a pair of life-sized plaster statues from their cabs. There on the pavement stood two hideously overdeveloped Grecian maidens, very chipped and quite awful.

When the joke was over, I wrote to Emile: "My mother says never accept statues from strange men, only jewellery." I tried to return them, but Emile refused to have them back. They were eventually removed to the prop room under the Ambassadors Theatre, where, for all I know, they still are.

On the day the war ended, the management told us that at the final curtain we would sing the English and American national anthems, also the French and the Russian.

The theatre was full of American troops and I realised that although we could get away with mumbling the words of the French "Marseillaise", and that no one would expect us to know the Russian, we had to sing the American national anthem

102

correctly. I think we all knew the first line and after that it was all la, la, la and every man for himself.

I explained our plight to Commander Longshore of the American Navy who had come round with some nylon stockings and a strapless bra that his mother had sent as requested. He never thought of telling her they were not for him.

"Fritz," I said to him, "we've got to sing the American anthem and we only know the opening words."

"Hermione, don't worry. The Navy's got the first six rows and we'll sing the words loud and clear; you just follow us." After the final curtain, I made a short speech: "Following the English national anthem, we will sing the national anthems of our brave allies."

Now I don't know how many people realise it, but "God Save the King" has the same tune as the American song "My Country 'tis of Thee". We had half the audience singing their version while we were singing ours.

"And now," I said, "we'll all sing the American national anthem."

The Americans stood to attention and the first line or two was splendid. After that it gradually drifted downhill into la, la, la's. No one remembered the words except for a black Army sergeant who sang practically solo.

Well we Allies won the war, though it seems winning a war is not all that it used to be. For the losers are doing very nicely, thank you, while poor old England . . . ? London, which I grew up in and which I shall always love, has risen from the ashes like a bird with motley feathers—which does nothing to enhance her appearance. It seems as if the London town planners finished Hitler's work for him.

Soon after the armistice *Sweetest and Lowest* closed. I shall always remember the last night. When I think of it, I wonder how I could have left the English theatre that meant so much to me, to start all over again; and never, I feel, achieve the same status.

I have found a very old copy of *The London Evening News*, and so I think if I quote from that, I shall at least get my facts right. It says the revue played to 800,000 people; that I played 1,676 performances; and that my dresser Kitty never missed one of my 17,010 changes. I had an average of sixteen changes in each show. I had so many costumes that my dressing room was too small to hold them all and I had to have another room just to keep the changes in. Mostly they had to be done at the side of the stage because we didn't have time to get back to the dressing room before my next entrance. Kitty was wonderful and ruled me and my visitors with a rod of iron. I remember her turning Prince Philip out of my dressing room—where he and Lord Milford Haven were waiting for the show to end because they were taking two of the girls out—saying, "If you must wait, wait in the corridor."

When he got engaged to Princess Elizabeth a short time later, I teased Kitty. I said, "He'll probably have you beheaded," which worried her for weeks. On the last night of the show, I brought Kitty onstage to take a bow, because without Kitty there wouldn't have been any show.

That last night of *Sweetest and Lowest* made theatrical history. One GI flew three thousand miles from Boston, and more than fifty fans queued all night. The police had to be called in to control the crowds. The narrow street outside the theatre was blocked with people clamouring for tickets. I talked to several of them. One man told me he'd seen our revue fifty times. I sent over to the Ivy and ordered drinks and food to be taken out and served to the fans. I think a lot of tears were shed on that last night. It was the end of an era. I sobbed and sobbed when that curtain came down.

Alan Melville came on to the stage to take a bow with us and I remember turning to him, my eyes full of tears, and saying, "They say you'll never write for me again."

"And it's true," he blubbed.

Poor Alan, I had pruned his material to suit my own personality. Of course, he did write for me again. He also wrote about me and I was very touched by his words.

I speak in very real gratitude when I say that an author lucky enough to write for Hermione knows that however good a line he might give her, some unexpected bonus will be added to make it sound better . . . a leer, a mangling of pronunciation, a signalled implication of double-entendre. She could, when occasion demanded it, persuade an audience that she was glamorous, even beautiful; and she had the true artist's gift, after making a packed house weak with laughing, of being able to still it in seconds when a touch of pathos was called for.

I am grateful for Alan's kindness and I would like to say that I owe him a great deal for all the marvellous material he has written for me over the years.

After three solid years of the *Sweet and Low* series, I badly needed a holiday. Now that the war was officially over, it was just possible to go abroad again—if one pulled strings. I managed to acquire two sleeper tickets for Italy in the names of Mr and Mrs Newman. Armed with Charles Hickman and eight pounds of coffee, courtesy of the US government PX, I set off to get to Capri or bust. It was nearly bust. The coffee was vitally important to use for bribes in case of awkward situations, and awkward situations were rife. No sooner had we climbed into our couchettes for the night than the Belgian customs flung open the door to our compartment and demanded to see our tickets.

"Thank you, Mrs Newman—and now your passport please?" he said in French. I fumbled under my pillow and reluctantly handed him my passport and watched his face turn purple as he read "Hermione Ferdinanda Maschwitz, known as Gingold". I'd be the first to admit it's the last name you'd use if you were writing a novel about an international spy—it would just be too obvious. In my best French, I told him that Mr Newman would explain. Charles handed over his passport and as the customs man started yelling, "Ce c'est le passport de M'sieur Charles Hickman? Ce n'est pas regulaire," I got out two pounds of coffee and smiling my most bewitching smile, I waved them under his nose. The poor man had obviously been drinking acorns for eight years, for as the aroma of real coffee reached his nostrils, his manner changed. I batted my eyelids innocently—"Café?"—and watched the packets disappear into the folds of his cloak.

"Bon soir, M'sieur-Dame." He saluted and with the suggestion of a leer, called "Dormez bien," as he pulled our door closed again.

Two days and nights later, we were out of coffee but we had reached Naples. We crossed to Capri, where we had two delicious weeks. The American troops had been using Capri as a rest centre, but they had gone and the tourists hadn't yet discovered it. Even Gracie Fields hadn't yet discovered it. It was heaven. The war seemed hardly to have touched it—although sometimes as we sat in the piazza, an old lady dressed in black would shuffle across the square and elbows would nudge. In whispers she would be pointed out as "Il Duce's mama".

The closing of the show left a great gap in my life. I made a few films, *The Butler's Dilemma*, a comedy with Richard Hearne; *Our Girl Friday*; and *Cosh Boy*, a nice family picture that was called *The Slasher* in the United States. The star of this film was Joan Collins and I believe I played her daughter. Although on second thought, she may have been playing *my* daughter. Anyway, I feel sure we were related. Joan was twenty and very beautiful. It was one of her first films, but she was already very much the star. She seemed to be under the constant protection of her father, and he wouldn't let anyone sit near her, let alone with her, in the studio canteen.

I was new to filming and didn't care for it much. Television I cared for even less. I only did one early television programme. I went up to a studio at Alexandra Palace in North London, from where television was transmitted live. The studio was in utter chaos; no one seemed to know what they were doing, but as no one was watching—there being about five sets in the country at the time—it didn't matter very much. I was shown into a roastingly hot little room with a tin box in it and I was warned not to "fall out of the picture". I had been made up to have a yellow face, blue eyebrows, and purple lips. I was told these bizarre additions would make my face come across better.

As my face, even with the makeup, looked nothing more than a flickering blur, I completely lost interest in anything to do with television. I boldly told my friends, "It will never catch on."

Now the war was over, I felt it was safe enough to retrieve my furniture from Brian's barn at "Wardrobes". I moved to 85 Kinnerton Street—it was only two doors along from 81, but it had a garden and was for rent, unfurnished.

My maid and cat never returned from the country, but for different reasons. My maid didn't want to come back to London and my cat had died.

I tried to find a replacement maid, but finding staff was never again to be easy and inexpensive as it had been before the war. Eventually, I ended up with a handsome young Italian man-servant who boasted references from Peggy Guggenheim in Venice. As these were scribbled on copybook paper, they didn't look too convincing; but as I was at my wits' end, I engaged him. Strangely enough, he turned out to be superb and his only fault was that whenever I had a cocktail party, all my gay male friends

107

would congregate round him in the kitchen. He left after three months because he found he couldn't stand the English climate.

I never had another cat, but Eric gave me a dear dog whom I called Mr Poodle. Mr Poodle had been an actor. He played the part of a dog. It was quite a major part in Eric's musical *Paprika* and Mr Poodle stopped the show with his "singing". Unfortunately, his song drowned out the dialogue of the other actors and he was replaced after the first night. He tried to overcome his theatrical rejection by settling for a quiet life chez Hermione, but I knew he was still hankering to tread the boards and he was soon given another chance. I made a rather bad B film called *Master Crook* in which I played a lady of easy virtue who was walking through the dark London streets when she was set upon by robbers and rapists. She was supposed to have a dog with her who defended her from the attackers and made them run away.

"Oh, Mr Poodle can do that," I told the director. "It will come quite naturally to him."

But his repertoire proved to be limited. When the robbers attacked me, Mr Poodle wagged his tail like mad and appeared to be egging them on.

Mr Poodle assured me he just hadn't found the right part, and he almost got another break later in America when I played in *The Sleeping Prince*. I tried to get him the part of the dog in the play, but a Borsoi beat him out of the role. The Borsoi had a better agent. I knew America was the country for me when I discovered that dogs had agents.

Dear Mr Poodle, he was a wonderful dog—he thought he was a person and sometimes I think I am, too.

I was very happy at 85 Kinnerton Street. Charles Hickman moved into my old house—"Club 81"—Brian took a lease on 83, and Chris Hewett was at 80, so I was surrounded by friends. Kinnerton Street in peacetime was delightful and we renamed it "The Village". There was a wonderful "Village Stores" in the street, where a dear lady seemed to play at shops. Rumour had it that every morning she went to Harrods, which is very near Kinnerton Street, where she bought fresh food to stock her shop. She'd sell you a quarter of Harrods best ham for two pence less than she'd paid for it. Her other foible was that when she chose not to sell you something, she'd speak politely in a near whisper.

"Oh, I'm sorry, I can't sell you that box of matches; it's the last in the shop and someone else might want to buy it."

I loved "The Village" and yet London wasn't the same for me. It had come to represent fear, and at night I couldn't look up at a clear moonlit sky without thinking, "What a lovely night for a raid." Also, my American chums had trickled back to the States and I missed them terribly.

Although the show had finished, I had plenty of work; and the BBC, reneging on their vow never to employ me again, gave me a weekly radio show of my own called "Home at Eight". Part of it was "Mrs Doom's Diary". Sid Colin, who wrote "The Dooms", did us proud. He managed to combine the silly and bizarre in a way that just appeals to my sense of humour.

"The train now standing at platform Number One is for Birmingham, Vladivostok, Puerto Rico, Greed, Avarice, Low Cunning, and all stations to Oblivion."

It obviously appealed to others as well, for the show rose to the top of the ratings. I played Drusilla, the mother of the bizarre family. We opened one episode with my knitting:

"One plain, two purl, one plain, two pearls, one diamond, two spades, three no trumps. I'm making a woolly jumper for my brother Walter who lives in Regents Park."

"But Drusilla the sleeves reach almost to the ground. You obviously don't know much about knitting."

"You obviously don't know much about my brother in Regents Park."

"Last week Drusilla surprised us all by running up a pair of curtains—a little trick she learnt in her circus days."

The show always ended with my pouring tea for my husband, Edmond, and saying, "Tea, Edmond? Mulluck?"

This came to be the new pronunciation for *milk*. Alfred Marks played Edmond, my husband, and we had a butler called Trog who was only ever heard as heavy footfalls. Our son was played by Dickie Attenborough who, years after, became Sir Richard Attenborough and directed *Gandhi*. It was outrageously funny—Mrs Doom, I mean, not *Gandhi*—and a great success.

Sid also wrote "A Date with Hermione". Each episode began: "Have you met Hermione Gingold? You should, you know—she's fabulous."

I'd make an impressive entrance but then end up in some sort of ridiculous situation at the Cannes Film Festival or at a theatrical garden party working on the white elephant stall—"I've sold myself three times already."

It usually ended with some sort of put-down such as: "I wouldn't say Hermione tries to attract attention, but the other day in Bond Street, the crowd was so big they almost knocked her off her stilts."

With success came some treats—such as an invitation to the Royal Garden Party. I was thrilled and took all day to get ready. I was so excited that when the time finally came for me to take a taxi to the Palace, I forgot my invitation card. Although I bumped into some friends at the Palace gates who said they were prepared to swear I was the genuine Hermione Gingold, I could see an aide-de-camp was scrutinising the invitations and my sense of protocol impelled me to return home at once and get my invitation.

I loved the garden party and watched as the gentlemen-at-arms formed lanes among the crowds so the Royals could walk along and meet selected guests. I decided not to join the lanes but stood on a little hillock and watched from afar. Prince Philip spotted me standing alone and I was flattered when he recognised me and came over smiling.

"What are you doing here?" he asked.

"I was about to ask you the same question," I retaliated.

Among the other guests, I was delighted to find Eric. Of course, by now we were divorced and he was married. I was doing well and financially I was quite well-off, but not by Eric's standards. He was having phenomenal success with his musicals, and royalties from "A Nightingale Sang in Berkeley Square" and "Room Five-Hundred-and-Four" were rolling in. In fact, he was doing so well that I broached a tender subject. "Eric, darling, what about some alimony?"

"Oh no," he said, "I could never take money from a woman." His reply made me laugh so much that I let him off.

Later I was invited to another garden party, this time at Number 10 Downing Street, which I was surprised to find has a large garden behind it. I enjoyed the party greatly, but I'm afraid I rather blotted my copybook when, on my way out, a journalist asked me what I thought of the party. "I loved it," I told him truthfully, "but the cakes were stale," which they were. Unfortunately, he splashed HERMIONE GINGOLD FOUND DOWNING STREET CAKES STALE all over the papers. Bang goes my OBE, I thought. I was rather embarrassed at sounding so ungrateful, but it taught me a valuable lesson on how careful you have to be when making a casual aside to a member of the press.

S uccess also brought burglars. The press began to call me "the most burgled actress in London". My first burglary was the worst. The burglar actually rang up three days before he struck to say "we're burglaring you on Friday". I thought it was a joke and took no notice—until I went home on Friday to a very cold and empty house. The crook must have had some conscience, for I'd left my gas fire on and he turned it off for me. He also took my engagement book and I felt the least he could do was ring up to tell me what my engagements were that week, but he didn't. By the time the sixth burglar struck, there was nothing left to take but a bar of soap and my ration book—so he took them, along with half a bottle of cooking sherry. It left a nasty taste in my mouth.

I performed in one more revue in England, *Slings and Arrows* at the Comedy Theatre. Wally Crisham was my leading man again. Charles Hickman and I devised the show between us and I wrote part of the show myself, as well as "discovering" some new writers who went on to join Alan Melville and Herbert Farjeon in the ranks of the great revue writers. One was Peter Myers, who'd been writing at the tiny Chepstow Theatre, and the other a young man just down from Oxford named Sandy Wilson.

Peter Myers went on to collaborate with Ronnie Cass on *For Amusement Only* and *The Lord Chamberlain Regrets* and eventually for films such as *Summer Holiday* and *The Young Ones*. Peter wrote a delicious sketch for me about an extremely ugly and disgruntled masseuse.

I'm just a Masseuse, a Masseuse,
I've been pulling and pushing for years.

Sandy wrote a funny "deep gloom" number called "Sit down a minute, Medea", where I draped myself around a pillar, saying, "This is my personal column." He also wrote a number for Wally about a night watchman in the London of 1666. "Twelve o'clock and everything's ghastly", to which I contributed the throwaway

112

line: "Hush, hush, whisper who dares—Christopher Wren is designing some stairs."

Of course, Sandy went on to write that brilliant twenties pastiche musical *The Boyfriend*, but I believe it was *Slings and Arrows* that gave him his first foothold in the theatre.

My pet number in the show was Arthur Macrae's "Blanchisseuse Heureuse" (The Happy Laundress). It was inspired by high laundry prices. Arthur decided his laundress was living at the Ritz and for some reason he thought of me. I became his exquisitely evening-gowned laundress, ironing shirts in a diamond tiara, moistening the linen with champagne, and continually burning my customers' garments, making tiny holes in unfortunate places.

> *There's never a dull moment in the laundry*
> *For if things get quiet I don't just sit and fret,*
> *I crush pyjama buttons into fragments*
> *With these rather dainty Cartier casse noisettes.*

I also loved a spoof Covent Garden opera number where we pretended Elisabeth Schwarzkopf had a cough, so I was to sing Mimi. "We are nearer God's heart at 'The Garden' than anywhere else on earth."

Although we went into a second edition of *Slings and Arrows*, I was impatient to try my wings in America, and I began to plan a visit. Even though the war was over, it wasn't easy to get permission to leave England. I had to pull a lot of strings, the strings eventually reaching the First Lord of the Admiralty and finally the Minister of Transport, Alfred Barnes. The Minister brought it up in Parliament, where they said, "Oh yes, let her go"—and I expect they added "and good riddance, too".

Before I left England, something rather odd happened to me. I used to buy my hats from Otonos (not his right name, but I don't want to be involved in any unpleasantness). He was the most expensive wholesale milliner in London; all the best shops carried his labels. His hats were even sold in New York.

I was allowed to buy hats straight from him only because I worked in the theatre. I must say his hats were divine. He had a showroom in the West End and a workroom somewhere out of town, which the government took over during the war for the manufacture of small arms. (Perhaps it's unnecessary, but I'd like to state that the government was not investing in pygmies.) Otonos was German but a naturalised Englishman.

One night someone high up in our spy service went to my dressing room at the theatre and asked me to keep an eye on Otonos and report back if I thought he was doing anything suspicious, which was just my cup of tea because if I hadn't been an actress, I would have chosen to be a spy. However, my father had convinced me there was practically no future in it but the firing squad.

All I found out about Otonos was that he was gay, and that was common knowledge. Although I did discover that he used to entertain young RAF officers at his country house at weekends, where champagne flowed, which is nonsuspicious, he also gave gold cigarette cases away as presents. I reported back to headquarters that I thought the cigarette cases could have been given for knowledge obtained "under the influence" or for "services rendered". I fancied I discerned a hint of sarcasm when my high-up said, "Thanks a lot."

Being naturally mad about hats and reluctant to relinquish my secret agent role, I continued to patronise Otonos without occurrence, until my farewell visit one afternoon just before I sailed for America. After I had chosen two particularly divine hats for myself, Otonos asked me to step into his inner office, where he looked at me in a quizzical way and said, "Would you do me a great favour? Would you take two hats to a milliner in New York for me? They will be packed in separate hatboxes from yours and labelled so you won't open them by mistake.''

I agreed readily and said I would be only too glad to help him, and in return he refused to let me pay for my own hats. I was absolutely thrilled and couldn't wait to hurry the hatboxes round to my high-up in the spy service. I rushed them round with a certain amount of caution, as I was convinced the boxes contained bombs designed to blow up the ship. I already had visions of getting the bombs defused and the ship saved, whereupon my Downing Street indiscretion would be forgiven and I would be summoned to Buck House again, where I would be decorated by the Queen and become a heroine as well as a star.

You can imagine my disappointment when I asked my high-up: "What was in the boxes?" He said, "Hats!" He returned the boxes and I carried them—as requested—to America.

I left for America with my dreams of heroism shattered and only five pounds in cash, as this was all the currency regulations would allow me to take out of the country.

I was the only civilian on board except for war brides and babies. Luckily, one of the officers gave up his bedroom to me. The ship rolled all the way to New York and took eight days, as we were continually dodging the mines that hadn't been swept up yet. I stayed in bed for the whole voyage.

The day after reaching New York, I took the hats to the address on the label. There two men greeted me with delight, grabbed the hatboxes, and said, "Do see if there's anything in the showroom you like and, if so, we'd be delighted if you would accept it." And so saying, they disappeared into the back office. After a minute, one of the men returned. He was pale and angry.

"These hats have been unpacked," he cried.

Before I could think what to say, the other man came in, whispered something in his ear, and they both disappeared into the back office. After a few minutes, they came back again, all charm and graciousness, and said, "Found anything to suit you?" I thanked them and said I had more than enough hats and lied that I hardly ever wore them. Then we all shook hands and I

115

returned to where I was staying, wondering what it all meant. I never did get to the bottom of it. I'm sure it couldn't have been important, as the war was over and we had won, and there I was in the city of my dreams with a new life in front of me.

2

AMERICA:

"America, God Shed His Grace on Thee . . ."

As the SS *United States* pulled into the dock in New York, the first thing I saw was a big placard saying WELCOME HERMIONE. It was held aloft by about two hundred friends and servicemen, which surprised me because I hadn't written to anyone to say I was coming and I hadn't been sure of the trip till the last minute.

"What's the first thing you would like to do?" they asked. Obviously, I couldn't tell them and instead said, "I'd love a banana split."

We left my luggage at the Ocean Terminal and a little group of us went straight to Rumpelmayers. I hadn't had a banana split for five years, and wanting to make up for it, I had not one but three in quick succession and began to feel very sick.

We collected my baggage and took it to Jimmy Morcome's apartment where I was to stay. That evening I recovered enough to go out to dinner and I ordered steak. When the steak arrived, it was so large that I burst into tears—in England a steak that size would have been the week's meat ration for a family of six.

I don't remember much about my first week in New York. I made quite a hit with the American press by saying how much I loved the large statue of Judith Anderson at the entrance to New York harbour. Then I think I spent most of the time eating or in bed. Later I do remember meeting a woman who said how dreadful the war had been for the American civilians. "I wasn't able to water my garden for two months," she said. I felt as though I was in a different world.

While I was at Jimmy's, a telegram arrived from Noël Coward asking me whether I'd be interested in going back to England to co-star with Totie Baddeley in a revival of his play *Fallen Angels*. Although I didn't relish the prospect of working with Baddeley again, I hadn't done a stage play, as opposed to a revue, for seven years and the idea of sustaining a character through three acts appealed; but Noël wanted me to play the part of Julia. I cabled: "Would like to do *Fallen Angels*, but to play Jane as I think she's funnier." Another cable arrived from Noël, saying: "Julia much bigger part. It is the pivot of the show."

I cabled back: "Darling, quite agree Julia is pivot but I don't see myself pivoting. Other lady much funnier. Respect for your judgment unchanged as always but my head is that of a pig."

I have absolutely no recollection of Noël's reply, but I know it was rude. However, he said yes, and I rushed back, having paid for my trip to America by doing a sketch on TV with Ed Wynn in his "Four Star Revue".

It was my first American TV appearance, but it wasn't very memorable. The sketch "Careless Lives" was one I'd done in England and I knew it had to be played straight. Ed put on funny makeup and played it for laughs, which was fatal.

*F*allen Angels was put on by Peter Daubeny, who never came to watch rehearsals. The other producers, Charles Russell and Lance Hamilton, not only came to rehearsals but helped Willard Stoker with the direction. They were keen to keep the play as a period piece and dress it in the fashions of 1925, whereas I felt it was essential to update it. It was then becoming popular to bring Shakespeare forward in time; *Hamlet* had just been done at the

Old Vic in Victorian costume, so I suggested we reverse the process and dress *Fallen Angels* in the fashions in vogue at the time of the Druids. That project so worried them that they were only too thankful to agree to playing it in modern dress. I got my way and Molyneux designed me a stunning contemporary evening dress.

We opened at Stratford-upon-Avon when the Shakespeare Festival was over, which I thought was asking for trouble, but we were an enormous success. Willard gave Totie and me a certain amount of freedom to update the play. We didn't change a single line of course, but we built up some very funny business to liven up the second act where two Mayfair ladies are supposed to get rather tight on champagne while awaiting their French lover.

In the twenties two ladies getting drunk was considered shocking, but we had to go further to create the same impact in the fifties. Totie invented some business with a bread roll. I think she was spitting out bits of it, which to my mind was a little vulgar, but the audience seemed to love it. I picked up a shiny dinner plate and used it as a vanity mirror, and when I dropped my napkin and tried to beckon it up off the floor, the audience went into near hysterics.

The pre-West End tour had reached Plymouth before Noël put in an appearance. As soon as he began to receive rather large royalty cheques, he rushed down to see a performance.

When the first-act curtain was lowered, Noël stormed on to the stage and proceeded to tell my co-star what he thought of her performance. Then he turned on me, but before he could open his mouth, I stopped him and with all the dignity I could muster said, "If you have anything to say to me, say it in my dressing room and not in front of the stagehands." And I walked off. I can't tell you how brave that was, because we were all terrified of Noël. Noël followed me to my dressing room and apologised but wagged his finger at me and said, "Now, Boodles"—Boodles was the childhood nickname he always called me by—"Now, Boodles, don't go too far."

I explained that I found his play old-fashioned and I was going

121

as far as I thought the play could stand. Although he still tried to alter bits here and there, I said, "No, dear, it's too late, it goes to London as it is," and we parted the best of friends. He even sent a rather sweet telegram later admitting we were right and he was wrong.

In London we opened at the Ambassadors Theatre. Totie and I were apprehensive of entering the stage door. We both knew there was only one stage-level star dressing room at the Ambassadors and although the question of who should have the star dressing room had never been raised, we each knew it was on the other's mind. By fate—or design, I don't remember which—we both arrived at the stage door together and the stage-door man handed us each a key to dressing room number one. In surprised silence, we descended to the dressing room and found not one but two stars pinned upon the door. This was too much—surely it wasn't proposed that we co-habit? Sparks flew from our keys as they clashed against each other trying to be first in the lock. I forget whose key did unlock the door, but it opened to reveal —that tiny theatre dressing room with a rough brick wall erected down the middle, effectively dividing it into two. It was Charles's and Lance's idea and oh, how it made us laugh!

After that we knew the show had to be a success and it was. The critics said we were very naughty ladies; they called us "gorgeous gargoyles" and said we had burlesqued Noël's play but admitted they loved every minute of it, saying, "The results were what the twenties would have called a wow!" The audience agreed and we ran for over a year. I admit we were naughty, but we must have been right, for it was subsequently revived with Constance Cummings playing it as a straight drawing-room comedy and it was not a success; and an American revival pairing Baddeley and Joan Blondell opened and closed so fast it created a vacuum.

When I said I wanted to leave *Fallen Angels*, the show closed, and my co-star went on tour in *Diary of a Nobody*. I think she wrote it herself. It's strange how Hermione Baddeley went to America, too—in the end.

Perhaps I have been a little cruel about Totie, but then she was unjustly cruel about me in her autobiography. My original idea was to take my revenge on her by not mentioning her once by name in this book—I knew nothing would upset her more. But perhaps one should let bygones be bygones. Despite our ups and downs, I remember the great fun we had, and hearing of her death recently saddened me more than I can say.

My ambition was still to do a revue on Broadway, so I rushed back to America hoping to fulfil my dreams. I found the Theatre Guild was interested in doing a revue for me. Most members of the Guild had seen *Sweet and Low*, but they asked me to sing some numbers to those members who hadn't. It was in effect to be an audition.

A really good accompanist is essential for any singer, but especially important to anyone performing subtle comedy material. In London my pianist, Clarry Ashton, had worked hard to familiarise himself with my every change of tempo and mood; he could play a chord in the perfect place to enhance a comedic effect; the same chord half a beat too soon or too late can kill a gag stone dead. Sadly, Clarry was in London, but it so happened that my current boyfriend was a classical pianist. However, a classical pianist does not necessarily make a good accompanist. He was sure he could accompany me beautifully. I had reservations but didn't like to hurt him by trying to find a more experienced substitute. I paid a high price for sparing his feelings, for I took him along to play for me but after two numbers, I realised it was a hopeless attempt and the whole thing fell through.

I'd learnt my lesson and I set about making a professional long-playing gramophone record of my best revue numbers. It was called "La Gingold—life of the party!" Although at the time it didn't make me much money, it has now become quite a collector's item. I'm so glad I made it, as it is the only sound recording of my revue appearances. It has reaped me untold benefits, because radio stations seem to have it and are always playing some snippet or other from it when they present nostalgia comedy programmes.

Although the Theatre Guild revue was off, I was fortunate in having another offer. Beatrice Straight and her husband liked my work and believed Broadway would, too. Beatrice offered to give me a flat and a play. The flat was most important as I still wasn't allowed to take much money out of England; in fact, I was practically penniless. Jimmy Morcome said I was welcome to stay with him as long as I liked because I had put up with him during the war, but I wanted a place of my own, so the flat was appetising bait.

The play *Lilly Henry* had promise. Although the last act hadn't been written, the first half was very funny and I flew to Bermuda with my pianist boyfriend to work on the first act.

I worked hard in Bermuda but I had fun, too. We were lent a house on the coast with its own little harbour and speedboat. We used to take the boat out to deep water and picnic and swim off the side of the boat. We then discovered the waters were infested with barracuda who would follow the big ships going into Hamilton and feast off the rubbish that was tossed overboard. We soon ceased our offshore bathing and returned to New York in one piece.

I settled into the new flat Beatrice Straight had found me. It was on Sixty-fourth Street, a few doors down from Fifth Avenue. It was an old brownstone that had originally belonged to the Roosevelts or Rockefellers. I had the ground-floor rear flat, which had originally been the library and had now become a sitting-room. There was also a small bedroom, kitchen, and a bathroom. Beatrice Straight had furnished it very nicely for me.

Unfortunately, the building was bitterly cold, for the heating always seemed to be breaking down; but I didn't mind too much, as living there was enormous fun because of the extraordinary assortment of people inhabiting the rest of the block.

The front flat housed Thomas Schippers, and on the first floor in a tiny flat lived a German lady, the Baroness Von Zenderhurst, and her daughter. The baroness always wore a monocle and shared a divan bed with her daughter. When in passing I asked the daughter what she wanted for her birthday, she said, "A horse."

The deteriorating Princess of Thurn and Taxis lived upstairs. She heard my chums had not only clubbed together to give me a winter coat but also a bottle of brandy, so every day she used to climb down from the sixth floor and go into a faint outside my door, where she'd lie like a little fluttering bird, calling, "Brandy, brandy."

Then there was the flautist, whose name I've forgotten, who could only play his flute when stripped to the waist, so he could never get any public engagements. He and I became quite pally, though I never heard him play. He did my shopping for me. Neither of us had much money and he sometimes stole steak, which I found frightening. I begged him not to do it, but he explained that it had become a habit that it would take some time to break.

The basement was occupied by a young married couple. I was told they were both very handsome, but I never saw them. I believe they spent all their time in bed. The wife eventually committed suicide.

When rehearsals began for *Lilly Henry*, they didn't go very well. Partly my fault, I'm afraid. I kept on asking when the last act was going to arrive, and ten days before we were to open, it still hadn't come. Beatrice Straight decided to cut her losses and call the whole thing off.

Another show that never came to fruition was Sandy Wilson's musical version of Cecil Beaton's *My Royal Past*. I was keen to do it because I liked Sandy so much. Anita Loos wanted to put it on and I was to co-star with the MGM singing star, Jeanette MacDonald —she playing the Grand Duchess Maria-Hedwig and I Baroness Hilda von Bülop. It all seemed promising until the first read-through. The script was very funny and Sandy had given us both lots of witty lines. Jeanette had been a big film star. She sang beautifully as she stood among the earthquake ruins in *San Francisco*, but a stage comedy actress she was not. At the script read-through, nearly all her funny lines were received in stony silence while the assembled company went into overkill on greeting my lines with guffaws of laughter. I knew it was spoiling for trouble and I tried to make my lines as deadpan and express-ionless as I could, which only seemed to make the cast laugh more. At the end of the first act, Jeanette looked very unhappy and refused to speak to me. We broke for coffee and Anita Loos surreptitiously took as many of the cast aside as she could and told them to stop laughing at me and start laughing at Jeanette. The read-through of the second half was slightly better; the cast tittered politely at Jeanette's lines and continued to roar at mine, but the damage was done.

Jeanette sent Sandy a telegram complaining that he'd given me too many witty lines and consequently she was withdrawing from the production.

The cast and I were put on standby while Anita and Sandy made futile attempts to get Jeanette to reconsider. I even offered to swap parts with her, but it's not for nothing that Jeanette was known in the profession as "the Iron Butterfly". Anita and Sandy tried to find a replacement for her, but they needed a star name. I wasn't established enough in America to carry the show on my own. It proved impossible to find another star at short notice. I was sad for the others in the cast, but the production seemed doomed and reluctantly I withdrew as well and the whole project was cancelled. In some ways, I was glad as I still felt that for my first appearance in New York, I should be in a revue.

Since this seems to be turning into a section on shows I never did, I'd like to mention a revue Boris Karloff and I were planning to do together in the sixties. I liked Boris enormously; in reality he was kind and gentle and not at all like the parts he usually played. We'd worked together twice in the past, doing a sketch in *A Night of a Hundred Stars*, and in Hollywood in a TV drama called *The Sting of Death*. We both thought a revue together would be very exciting. Boris felt the revue should be called *The Monster and I*, but never wanting to take second billing, I favoured the title *I and the Monster*.

What naughty teasers some of my enemies can be. Those who said that *The Monster and I* meant Boris had second billing were soon replaced.

Boris and I got film offers and we postponed our revue to the oblivion of shows that might have been. Sad, because I think a revue with Boris would have been enormous fun.

My new career in America didn't seem to be getting off to a very good start. Then I met Mary Hunter, who wanted to put on a revue called *It's About Time* at the Brattle Theatre in Cambridge, Massachusetts. She was going to use some of my English material, as well as several new American numbers.

I thought it would be better for me to do that than to do nothing. I also knew that John Murray Anderson was planning a revue and I thought I would lure him to the Brattle to see the show and me. So off to the Brattle I went and luck went with me.

The cast for *It's About Time* was first-rate and included Ronnie Graham and Muir Matheson. The new material was good and Walter Crisham appeared from nowhere and directed the whole revue, in the style of our English ones.

I remember three days before our first night, *The King and I* opened in Boston. I dashed over to see it and rushed back to write a parody of it with David Rogers. We called it *I and the King*, quickly rehearsed it, and with me playing Anna, we inserted it into *It's About Time*. It stopped the show. Richard Rodgers came to see our first matinée and he has never spoken to me since, which proves how successful it was.

John Murray Anderson came to the Brattle, liked the show and me, and asked whether I would co-star with Billy de Wolfe in his new Broadway show, which was to be called *John Murray Anderson's Almanac*.

Almanac was going to take several months to put together, so when I had an offer from Major Donald Neville Willing in London to do cabaret at the Café de Paris, its limited run was tempting. I was to follow Marlene Dietrich, and that in itself was a challenge, so I cabled yes.

I had never done cabaret before, but I believe in trying everything once—except country dancing and incest.

Immediately, I rang Cunard to book my passage; unfortunately, as they had no free cabins, it seemed there was no alternative but to fly. I had always been terrified of flying and I began to tremble at the prospect. The dear doctor I had then decided the best thing for me would be to sleep the entire journey.

"It's a nonstop flight—you'll fall asleep and when you wake up, you'll be in England," he reassured me. "I'm going to give you an injection that would put an elephant to sleep." It probably would have, but I am not an elephant.

I did drop off for about five minutes while we got airborne and I woke up just in time to see a dear boy come out of the pilot's cabin to show us his life jacket. He explained that if the plane ditched

Our dual poster . . . Hermione Baddeley and me in *Fallen Angels*

"They don't come to hear me play . . .
they come to see me walk away!"

"Ah yes, I remember it well." *Gigi*,
1958, with Maurice Chevalier

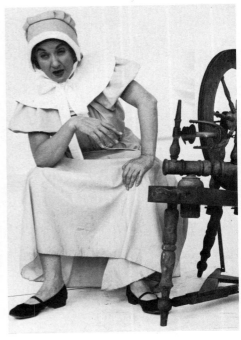

I had to keep a level head in Hollywood . . .

. . . but I still made all my own clothes.

We have to think our chin muscles up!

And it turned out all right for me and
Mr Poodle.

Me with Charlton Heston . . .   . . . Richard Burton

. . . Jerry Lewis   Hollywood had its compensations.

Nubar Gulbenkian, me, Paul
Getty. "Paul wants to know if
he can borrow a quarter."

"You'll get no quarter from
this old bag."

Below: Giving a birthday
tribute to Helen Hayes

Noël Coward and me giggling
our way to the land where the
rainbow ends

"Your seat's bigger than
mine!"

"This is your life." I'm seated
between my sons Stephen
and Leslie Joseph

Arriving in San Francisco to begin a new career in opera
with my dog Messey Missey

A Little Night Music, 1975

Glynis Johns and Len Cariou.
"When shall we three meet again?"

With Jean Simmons. She's charming, talented, beautiful . . . I should hate her.

Side by Side by Sondheim, 1979

With my goddaughter, Hermione Eyre, and her mother, Anne Clements Eyre. It's only Anne who would choose a godmother who isn't religious, hates children, and lives three thousand miles away.

I was 80 when this picture was taken . . . and I
haven't been touched up.

into the Atlantic, we would need them, and he instructed us on the intricacies of blowing them up. He then flourished a whistle on a long chain and said if we were in the sea, we could blow it to attract attention. Imagine—in the middle of the Atlantic!

The thought of floating among the waves hopefully blowing my whistle to attract all those sharks so terrified me that the elephant injection didn't work at all and I remained wide awake. Then the flight became very turbulent. In fact, it became so rough that I suspected we were already floating in the Atlantic and they hadn't liked to tell us; but no, they said that the turbulence was caused by strong headwinds and they announced that we would be making an unscheduled landing in Boston to take on more fuel.

"Good," I said, "I'm getting off."

"You can't get off," they protested. "This is a nonstop flight."

"But the pilots just said we're going to stop, and as soon as we do, I'm getting off," I insisted. The hostesses weren't at all pleased and didn't want to let me off.

"You can't get off," they reiterated, "and if you did, your luggage wouldn't get off with you."

"I don't care," I said, "if I have to stay on, I know I'll have hysterics."

That would scare off the other passengers they thought—a good reason to let me off, and my luggage, too. I went straight to a hotel and luckily got a bedroom, threw myself on the bed, and went into an elephantine sleep that lasted twelve hours.

I woke up deciding flying was strictly for the birds and I vowed then I would never fly again, and I never have.

I got the first possible train to New York and rang Cunard, who had a fully booked *Queen Mary* leaving for England the next day. I pleaded with them and eventually they said, "Bring your luggage and sit on the deck and if someone doesn't turn up, you can have their cabin."

I did just that and it worked because someone's maid didn't turn up and I was given her cabin—an inside one so small that my luggage had to stay outside the door. Dressing for dinner became almost as bad as the labours of Hercules. Luckily, it was a smooth crossing.

Meanwhile, in London, the press met the plane that I was supposed to be on, and when they asked what had become of me, they were told: "She got off."

"Got off—a *nonstop* flight?" They stood by, shaking heads and watching as my mink stole, which I'd left behind in my hurry to get off the plane, was carried off by a stewardess. I was told all this by friends who had also met the plane. Apparently one of them suggested that perhaps I'd transferred to a broomstick.

I think this is when I began to earn the quite unjustifiable misnomer of—the witch. For fun, Angus McBean took some photographs of me flying over London on a broomstick, but I'd like to point out to my readers that these pictures were faked. I'm not at all witchlike really, although I have been told that some people do find me frightening. I've never understood this at all. I'm intolerant of people who are stupid or rude, so perhaps at times I can be a little intimidating, possibly a little bitchy on occasion, possibly very bitchy, but frightening? A soft-centred generous soul like me? Surely not.

I was once asked, "Hermione, which is the real you?" My dears, if only I knew. How I envy schizophrenics with their personalities split neatly in two. I'm afraid I have at least six personalities, all constantly at war with one another and requiring to be housed, clothed, and fed according to their various needs. This makes life not only very confusing but astronomically expensive. First and foremost is the *actress* in me. Completely bound up in the theatre, she is affected and exotic, eats out a lot, doesn't get up till late afternoon, takes no exercise, and wears ridiculous hats. She lives in complete contrast to the *normal type* who gets up early, wears sensible clothes, no makeup, and spends a lot of time gardening and replying to letters by return post. Thank goodness she only appears at weekends. Then there is the *intelligent* personality. She appears at intervals and stays long enough to write a few chapters of a book and then disappears for quite a time. Frankly, she is my least favourite character, as she shuts herself away with pen and paper and never has any fun. She reads Proust, lives in an embroidered Russian blouse, has a permanent ink stain on her nose, and feeds solely on rye bread and yogurt. All my friends hate her, as she slams down the phone and refuses to go to parties. She is on the worst possible terms with the *femme fatale*, but you already know more than enough about *her*. She is loathed and despised by the *housewife* in me who occasionally takes it into her head to enter the kitchen and prove what a good cook she is. Of course, she never uses a cookery book—she cooks by ear; but she's practical and economical, although sometimes she goes too far and starts scrubbing the floor, putting up shelves, and, if she has to, changing a fuse. She is the only one on speaking terms with my *better self*, who has just arrived and told me to stop all this nonsense and get on with the story.

I reached England on my usual means of travel—ship. I caught the boat train to Waterloo, where a man with a microphone rushed up to me and said, "The BBC would like to interview you for 'In Town Tonight'."

Before I could say, "How much?" he nipped in neatly with, "The BBC would like you to accept a spray of flowers." Then I remembered that, unlike New York, it's bad form to bring up the subject of money with the BBC.

London was wildly exciting—there was a new issue of ration books and it was outsize coat week at Derry & Toms. I had no time to attend that thrilling event as I had to get my cabaret act together. It was lovely to work with Clarry Ashton again, and together with Miles Rudge, we worked every day and all day.

Dietrich had the splendid idea of getting a series of well-known celebrities to introduce her each night—I wish I'd thought of it first. However, I didn't want to repeat the idea, especially when I heard you had to buy the celebrities dinner at the Café by way of thanks; besides, if you're having an introduction, surely it's impolite not to introduce the person who's introducing you. This led to inspiration for my opening song: "Who's to introduce the introducer's introducer, for the introducer's introducer must be introduced."

The dress I chose for the opening was made by an actor from a drag revue that was playing in a tiny theatre in Leicester Square. I went to see it one night and the clothes were simply wonderful, so I went backstage to find out the dress designer's name. The leading "man" said he'd made them himself. I asked him whether he'd make me a copy of the one he wore in the finale and he said he'd be delighted.

"What about fitting?" I asked.

"Won't want any," he answered. "You and I have the same figure—just you leave it to me."

I didn't argue the point but told him it was for my opening at the Café. In order to make it less like a copy of his, we decided to subdue the colour to hot pink. It was delivered in time for the opening and not a stitch had to be altered. Eventually, I wore it in New York for the finale in *Almanac*.

At the Café de Paris, we had an afternoon dress rehearsal to which I invited the Gallery First-nighters. Major Donald Neville Willing (ever willing as always) arranged afternoon tea for them. They were most helpful and an excellent audience and it seemed as if I was going to be a hit.

132

The first night was wonderful; the audience loved me and so did the press. I was terribly nervous before going on and I might never have made it if it hadn't been for Noël Coward. He sent a card wishing me luck and the most enormous basket of flowers. When I undid the cellophane covering over the flowers, a furious bee flew out and started to attack me. Remembering *Fallen Angels*, I felt sure Noël had put it there on purpose. In fact, it was a godsend, for instead of trembling with nerves as I waited for "Miss Gingold, you're on", I had to catch the bee and see whether I could avoid being stung.

Noël was in the first-night audience and came straight around afterwards. As he approached me, he started wagging his finger, which terrified me. He always wagged his finger and you didn't know whether he was going to say "you are very bad" or "you are very good", because he used to wag the same finger to praise or chastise.

I was overjoyed on this occasion because he couldn't have been sweeter and he said, "Boodles, you were very very good." I thanked him for his praise and then thanked him profusely for the flowers, adding, "The bee was a touch of genius." Noël looked amazed and said, "What bee?" with such innocence that I never knew whether he'd ordered it to divert me or sting me, or indeed whether he had been responsible for it being there at all.

There was only one show a night, and after my appearance, I'd change and have tea, ham, and eggs on the balcony with Major Dolly Willy Nilly. The Café was very chic—you were only seated downstairs if you were in evening dress. Otherwise, you sat up in the balcony. Quite often royalty slipped in to watch the show from upstairs.

During the day I found time to do a BBC special called "Grande Gingold". Making his debut in the show was a young man named David Jacobs. I believe it was his first broadcast and, wanting to make a good impression with the studio audience, he was mortified to wake up on the day of the recording with a large red boil on his face. I didn't know that throughout the day his friends had been reassuring him that the eruption was hardly noticeable and convinced him that his disfiguring molehill was a practically invisible pimple. Then I arrived at the studio. I took one look at him and said, "David darling, what's this—leprosy?" Sometimes I wish Tact was my middle name instead of Ferdinanda.

On that visit I also made a gramophone record with Gilbert Harding. I was very fond of Gilbert. I believe he could be abrasive to some people, but I only ever found him gentle and charming. He was really the kindest of men. Our record had the great distinction of being banned by the BBC.

We both sang beautifully—on one side, "It takes two to Tango" and on the other, a musical version of the children's fairy tale "Little Red Ridinghood". This was the side that caused offence. Our song was called "Oh Grandma" and darling Gilbert and I were totally perplexed as to why we had been banned. Further investigation informed us it was because of two lines in "Oh Grandma" where Gilbert as the wolf said, "Hermione can I have you as a regular diet?" and I replied, "Yes Gilbert, but don't speak with your mouthful."

The irony of it was that the offending lines had been written by John Mills's sister Annette, who was well known at the time for her television puppet "Muffin the Mule", which was considered very suitable for infants. Our big bad wolf fable was also written for children, but the powers that be at the BBC saw fit to find something suggestive in our rendition. Of course, the ban made our record sales rocket and I can only hope that those who bought the record for the wrong reasons feel they got their money's worth.

Strangely enough, it was during this visit that I bumped into my first husband, Michael Joseph. He was lunching at the Caprice with his current wife and their son, Richard, who had a patch over one eye. We were very polite to one another. He explained that his son hadn't become a pirate but had a stye. I helpfully suggested he try an old folk remedy—"Tell him to rub it with an old wedding ring."

My month at the Café passed all too quickly. England was about to launch "National Road Safety Week", which means they get terribly cross if you run anyone over in the first few days. So I felt I had better hurry back to America, but not before Beaudoin had made his first appearance in my life. He was French, Canadian, young, blond and very handsome. I knew he wanted to go to bed with me, and since no one objected we began a long-lasting affair that we resurrect whenever physical proximity allows.

I returned to New York to begin rehearsals for John Murray Anderson's *Almanac* of 1953. I had to find a new place to live because now that *Lilly Henry* was not going to be done, I couldn't expect Beatrice Straight to go on giving me a flat. Lenny Strauss, later to become my business manager and friend, found me an unfurnished flat on East Fifty-fourth Street. He said if *Almanac* was a success, I could send for my goods and chattels from London.

My love life was also most satisfactory. I left Beaudoin behind in London, but now Jack Wallace, my American sailor friend, was back and we were together again. I don't know how I would have got through rehearsals without Jack.

Although I now had a flat, it was empty except for a bed, a bridge table, and a kettle, so I would stay with Jack. He cooked for me and generally looked after me, and oh, how I needed him!

Almanac was an exciting show in which to be starring. John Murray Anderson described it as "a musical harlequinade"; he wasn't in it himself but he devised and staged the whole show. Billy de Wolfe, Harry Belafonte, Polly Bergen, and Orson Bean were also in the cast.

Billy de Wolfe and I had several sketches together. I was alarmed when I first met him. "Oh, dear," I said, "I've never worked with a man who has a moustache before"; but in fact, Billy and I became great friends. I enjoyed working with him enormously, but I remember a very anxious time when we were well into rehearsals and the script for the sketches hadn't arrived. It was a long time since I'd played them in London and I needed to refresh my memory. Billy had never even seen the script, and in desperation I asked John Murray Anderson when we could expect it. Smiling calmly, he said, "I really don't know. They've gone to Rome to be blessed by the Pope."

Then I remembered that one of our producers was very religious, so I stopped agonising and said, "I hope the Pope has a sense of humour."

John Murray Anderson didn't worry about the sketches; he was only interested in the musical numbers. Cyril Ritchard, famous for his role as Captain Hook in *Peter Pan*, was supposed to be directing the sketches, but he and I didn't get on very well together.

One afternoon he arrived in my dressing room and told my dresser to get out. She looked surprised but started to go. I stopped her and said to Cyril, "I'll tell my dresser when I want her to leave the room and she stays till then." We didn't speak much after that, which was just as well because he wanted to alter a sketch I had played with great success in England. The sketch in question was "Orient Express" by Orford St John, and I knew exactly how it should go. It concerns two ladies who sip port wine from a thermos flask all the way to Istanbul and in the course of the sketch get very drunk. I thought it could be extremely funny if Billy would play the other lady with me.

It was only with great difficulty that I got Billy to play the part of a woman, for he had to shave off his moustache, and he didn't think that his "tomatoes" (as he called his girlfriends) would like it. However, at last he promised to shave it off and do the sketch. To find him something to wear, I took him to Bloomingdale's, where I got hold of a very helpful salesgirl in the larger ladies department.

Billy rather fancied a beige lace afternoon frock and he strode out of the fitting room to see what it looked like from a distance —in a long mirror. This was before he shaved off his moustache, and several lady customers practically fainted. So he came back in a hurry and we persuaded him that the frock was not right for travelling in a train; he settled for a suit with a fox-fur stole.

As a crowd had gathered outside the fitting room, our nice salesgirl got him a hat from the millinery department. Billy, who by then had entered into the spirit of the thing, got a round of applause when he left, but that was nothing compared to the first night Billy and I played the sketch and stopped the show.

The sketch ended with a blackout and no one ever takes a bow after a blackout; it just isn't done. We had already gone to our dressing rooms and changed out of our costumes when the stage manager came rushing along, pleading, "You must come back —they just won't stop clapping." We had to return to the stage and take bows in our dressing gowns. The same thing happened with our next sketch—"Dinner for One" by Lauri Wylie—and I believe that it was the first time on Broadway that sketches had stopped the show.

Another sketch that got a fantastic reception was "La Pistachio" by Billy Wells, in which I was BoBo, the queen of Montmartre. On paper the sketch was very amusing, but I knew that for my Broadway debut, amusing wouldn't get me noticed—I had to be hilarious. Fortunately, Billy was quite happy for me to alter bits here and there to suit my own style. For example, for my first line, Billy had written: "Mortimer, there's a terrible smell of gas!" He let me change this to "Mortimer, there's a terrible smell of old diamond bracelets." By inserting some business such as using champagne as cologne and cooling my foot in an ice bucket, the sketch developed and reached its full potential.

Almanac also included one of my all-time favourite revue songs; by Alan Melville and Charles Zwar, it's about an imperious theatrical grande dame who, on being offered a small part in a tour of *Macbeth*, demands, "which witch?"

Billy de Wolfe and I got more than a good press; one critic called me "the funniest woman in the world", and a picture of me as BoBo in "La Pistachio" appeared on the cover of *Life* magazine.

It was marvellous to be working again and to be in a big Broadway success. So many people came round after the show to say how much they enjoyed it. At that time I used to keep a visitors book, which had been signed by everyone from Marilyn Monroe to Yehudi Menuhin; unfortunately it got lost in one of my moves. I didn't use it as a burnt offering as I did my earlier album.

Working for John Murray Anderson was wonderful, too. Did I say wonderful? I should have said bizarre—well, wonderful and bizarre. He really was a most extraordinary man. He was born in Newfoundland, grew up in Scotland, went to school in Switzerland, and settled in New York to become an antique dealer, a dancer, a director, and then an entrepreneur. In his time, he'd staged aquacades, circuses, and twenty-nine Broadway musicals.

He never went to parties and he only broke this rule once in all the time I knew him. That is when I managed to lure him to a small gathering of friends in my apartment. He stayed until the gathering turned into a party and then left. Normally, he sat in his apartment at a long and lovely oak table with his white Persian cat and two telephones, and he knew—how I don't know—where every cast member was. We were all given nicknames, too. I was Miss Binky, and a friend of mine who used to take me to all the most exclusive restaurants was nicknamed "the Meal Ticket". Murray used to call him that to his face.

Before the first night of the show, I was very nervous. I always am, but I was more so than ever as it was my Broadway debut. Of all things, my haemorrhoids started to give me awful pain. Murray came to see how I was doing and found me in tears. He sent for a doctor he knew. "He's known as Dr Miracle," he said, "and will have you fixed in no time."

Dr Miracle arrived and gave me an injection that really did seem like a miracle, for within minutes, I was not nervous anymore and free of pain. He then became my doctor and cured me of low blood pressure; and whenever I felt down and depressed, I was up in the clouds when I left his office. He never liked you to tell him what was the matter. When I told him I'd hurt my foot and was afraid I might have sprained it, he said, "Don't tell me what's the matter with you; I don't tell you how to act," which was true. I hoped he wouldn't give me the same injection that he had for nerves, depression, and haemorrhoids, but he did. Then he started to give me injections in the lobes of my ears and the backs of my hands, and I felt it was time to leave him before he became a habit, and I did just that. Not long after, he was the subject of a red hot scandal.

Fortunately, I left in time. I've always been extremely cautious about what goes into my body. Apart from my naiveté in accepting Dr Miracle's medication, I've never taken drugs, nor would I. It's because I like to be in absolute control of my own body that I don't drink, although I do indulge in the occasional glass of champagne—about once every four years. My friends are always saying, "Hermione, four years must be up, couldn't we crack open a bottle?" I invariably tell them, "No, I've another six months to go."

Almanac was going splendidly. I loved New York, although I realised it was a tough city if you wanted success, but as it was, I was wined and dined and I loved every minute of it.

Lenny Strauss thought it was safe to send for my goods and chattels and Mr Poodle. When they arrived, Jack Wallace moved in with me and I got myself an agent called Baron Poland whose name gave rise to some pretty silly jokes. He has since retired. I now have Milton Goldman, my friend and agent for more than thirty years.

I've enjoyed many happy times with Milton and with Lenny. Once when I was staying with Lenny in his Fire Island home, his cook asked me, "How can I make an apple pie with a difference?" "Use peaches," I suggested helpfully.

I also began to get lots of offers for TV shows. Two of my earlier TV shows were an "Omnibus Playhouse" of *She Stoops to Conquer* with Michael Redgrave, and a show called *Toast of the Town*.

139

Pageant magazine worked out that in these two shows, I'd been seen by almost 50 million TV viewers. So many times more than had ever seen me in all my years on the British stage. It seemed incredible to me.

The TV show I did most often and liked most was *The Jack Paar Show*. Jack's was my first American TV chat show. He introduced me to the studio audience and the viewers and then told me, "You should be very lucky, for you're sitting in Zsa Zsa's seat."

Much to the audience's delight, I replied, "Zsa Zsa who?" But honestly, I didn't know.

From then on, I became a weekly guest on the show, and I found a new public. At first I was very nervous; the chat show world is very competitive and I knew that if I was going to be a successful chat-show guest, I had to be a bit different. Fortunately, for me that wasn't difficult.

Several years later, Zsa Zsa and I were on the *Merv Griffin Show*. Zsa Zsa was on before me with Xavier Cugat's wife, Charo. Zsa Zsa was being extremely unkind and catty to Charo; then I walked on holding my little dog and said to Merv, "I hope you don't mind my bringing my dog on, but it seems to me one more bitch won't make any difference." The audience responded with laughter and applause, though Zsa Zsa looked at me as if she could kill. Merv said he thought my remark would have to be cut from transmission, but the studio audience shouted him down. Zsa Zsa commented that she thought I would never be invited back on the show, but Merv has invited me back many times since.

Jack was very good to me. He used to call me his "irregular regular", and being a weekly guest on his show gave me a wonderful start in America. Jack was very talented and unusually attractive. His show was enormous fun to do, though sometimes it terrified me to be on it—it was so wild. Occasionally, Jack would get confused and talk himself into a corner, but the audience loved it when he did—it made him seem more human. I was amused to find that after a few appearances on Jack's programme, I was approached by several business companies who offered me inducements if I'd mention their name on the show. I always declined these offers, but my top offer was a mink coat if I'd casually drop the name "The Merchant Seaman's Loan and Beneficial Society" into my conversation with Jack. I turned them down, but I told Jack about my tempting offer. To my surprise he said, "You should have done it."

"Oh, come on Jack, how could I just drop a name like that into the programme?"

"Easy," said Jack, "All you'd have to do is say, 'Funny thing happened to me on the way to the Merchant Seaman's Loan and Beneficial Society'."

Of course by then it was too late, but if any representative from that company reads this book, I'd like them to know I'm prepared to reconsider their offer.

Merv Griffin I adored, too; he was the most unspoiled man of importance I ever met. He was always as charming to the boot-black as he was to the stars. My favourite moment on his show was when I was going to give him a recipe for chicken à la Gingold. For safe keeping, I put the recipe down the front of my dress and when the time came to give it to him, I couldn't find it. I was digging around my bosom trying to retrieve it when Merv asked, "Do you need help?"

"No," I growled, "I know my way around."

Another programme that contributed to my success in America was a rather silly TV show called *One Minute Please*. The object of the game was to talk for a minute on any given subject. Of course for a chatterbox like me, this was terribly easy. We were never "briefed" with the subjects beforehand and sometimes they were most peculiar ones. On my first show, I was asked, "Hermione, explain whale blubber."

I said, "I think it is awfully sad seeing whales blubber."

My next question was "What makes an orangutan beat its chest?"

My answer was "Exhibitionism and the fact that it has come from a hot country to a cold one and is suffering from bronchial pneumonia."

And on "puppy love" I said, "There have been many husbands treated like dogs because of puppy love."

After these contributions, they made me a "One Minute Please" regular.

Almanac had been running six months and looked as if it would easily enjoy six more. I'd been given the Donaldson Award for the best musical comedy debut and everything was wonderful.

Then quite suddenly, darling John Murray Anderson died and the show closed. On top of that, Jack Wallace, who had been posted abroad, told me that he wasn't coming back to me. I realised it wasn't my fault, but it didn't make it any easier to bear.

All my life I've needed either to be loved or to be working —preferably both. At that moment, work seemed easier to find than real love, so I thrust myself into a new revue called *Sticks and Stones*. It wasn't a success, and as I still had no lover in my life, I begged my then agent to get me a job—anything, even a guest appearance with an out-of-town repertory company. He gasped with horror at the suggestion and when I told him, "I've heard they pay enormous sums to engage visiting stars," he gasped again and said, "I'll look into it at once."

He fixed me up with quite a lucrative engagement to "guest" for a week playing in *Fallen Angels* at the Midfield Summer Stock Theatre. We don't have summer stock in England, so I'd no idea what I was letting myself in for.

To me, summer stock sounded like a recipe for a delicious soup, but I was to discover it can land you right in the potage if you're not careful. All the people mentioned here are real but have been disguised in order not to cause unnecessary suffering.

I packed my props and costumes and drove to the spot indicated on the road map. Although it was late afternoon, there wasn't a soul in sight. There wasn't, to my practised eyes, a theatre in sight either, but there was a noticeably large barn. As the sun was hot, I wandered into it, much to the annoyance of a flock of birds who had decided to hold a meeting there. They left under protest, cawing and muttering and doing unspeakable things to my hat; never again will I allude to them as our feathered friends.

I looked around and realised that this was it. This was the Midfield Theatre.

I was just about to get back in the car to drive home when in rushed a troupe of extraordinary young people, some in very short shorts and long earrings, some in very tight leotards with real fur-fabric hair bandeaux. Their faces were as white as the driven snow and their eyes heavily kohled—I mean the girls, of course. The men had beards, sweat shirts—and I do mean *sweat* shirts—sandals on their feet, and knives in their belts. They were all eating King Kones. I thought they might be some new religious sect. But no, it turned out that they were the theatre staff.

On seeing my slightly dazed look, one dryad detached herself from the others and oozed in my direction.

"Oh Miss Gingold, honey," she panted, "how awful we were not to be here to greet you, but I know you'll understand; we've been working all night taking down and setting up, and we just went into town to get an ice cream."

The stage manager came over. He appeared to be the oldest of them all (in fact, it made me quite melancholy to think that he would obviously never see twenty again) and he asked me whether I would like to see a sketch of the set they had designed for me. I said it might be as well, and while they searched for the set design, I met a boy holding a large shaggy sheepdog on a rope. He was introduced as "our lighting expert".

143

"Now how shall we light you?" he declaimed. "Best to show, and yet conceal, what nature has so generously given."

And he waved both his arms in the air and dropped the rope, and the large shaggy sheep dog took off for the road, followed closely by the lighting expert. I never saw him again.

"We haven't much lighting equipment," said Jim as if nothing had happened. "In fact, we've run out of pinks and blues, but we've masses of mauves and oranges."

"I don't mind how I'm lit," I lied, "just anything will do. Glow-worms, fireflies, anything. Now, if I could go and rest somewhere."

"The acoustics," said Jim, "are a bit tricky. You see, this wasn't really built for a theatre."

"You don't say," I gasped.

"And we are not far from the airport," he went on, "and at curtain time they come in for landings. There is an owl in the rafters that hoots occasionally and a skunk under the stage, and apart from some bats, there is really nothing to worry about."

"That's taken a weight off my mind," I said weakly, "and now if I could go somewhere and lie down."

Suddenly, a hamadryad wearing a man's shirt, a yachting cap, and an old tutu raced over clutching a scrap of crumpled paper. "We've found the set design," she exclaimed, and handed me a sketch of a log cabin obviously situated somewhere in farthest Alaska, where men are trappers and Mayfair is a million miles away.

"I do not wish to seem difficult," I said, "but I think you must have read the wrong script. The play I am doing is Noël Coward's *Fallen Angels*, and the whole action takes place in a Mayfair drawing room. That is according to Noël."

"But Miss Gingold," said the stage manager, "don't you feel this is different?"

"Yes, candidly I do," I replied.

"You see," he went on eagerly, "it gives you a challenge to work against a hostile background. You don't want to take the dreary, easy, commercial approach, do you?"

144

"No," I agreed halfheartedly, and I could already tell that this was the last approach I was going to be allowed to take. I stuck it out and I think I can honestly say it was one of the most unforgettable weeks of my life.

The cast worked with enormous enthusiasm and somehow I managed to cobble together a production that bore some resemblance, albeit slight, to Noël's play. A huge audience turned up and much to my surprise, no one asked for their money back. I returned to New York looking ten years older but at last I had done summer stock.

I was thrilled when the following season the Midfield Theatre invited me to join their company again; in fact, I hadn't been so thrilled since the first time Dorothy Kilgallen insulted me in her column.

With deep regret, I gladly declined their offer. I may sound old-fashioned but I do like to work in a nice comfortable theatre made of real bricks, with real running water, and a real staff of grown-up people. My next offer was to do just that; I was keen to see America, so I went on tour starring in *The Sleeping Prince* by Terence Rattigan. I hasten to add that I wasn't playing the Prince. The play was filmed as *The Prince and the Showgirl*. Nor was I playing the Showgirl. In our production, I was the Prince's mother, which is a large part in Rattigan's stage version. On tour, the Showgirl was played by a clever young dancer who'd done a couple of minor film parts. I thought she was extremely talented, but the management didn't want her because she wasn't a name.

"Who's ever heard of Shirley MacLaine?" they asked. I fought hard for Shirley to play the part and very good she was, too. In fact, she astonished me, for she seemed to know instinctively the things it took the rest of us fifty years to learn. On the billboards for the tour, her name came below mine, but within two years she was starring in *Around the World in Eighty Days* and I, along with the world and his wife, had a tiny cameo part.

The section of *Around the World in Eighty Days* that I was in was the London sequence. Mike Todd was the producer and I was a rather dubious lady of easy virtue in full Victorian costume,

145

complete with high button boots. The boots were very difficult to do up as no one in the wardrobe department had brought a buttonhook; at last the sun came out and we were able to start filming.

"I'm ready," I called, "but no one can do my boots up."

"I'll be able to do them," said Mike Todd, and the famous producer knelt down and did my boots up with the greatest of ease.

"Where on earth did you learn to button boots so easily?" I asked him.

"Well," said Mike, "once upon a time, I used to be a shoe salesman." To this day, I don't know whether he was serious or not.

Around the World in Eighty Days was adapted by S. J. Perelman from Jules Verne's novel, and his script won an Academy Award for being the best screenplay of 1957.

Perelman had seen me in *Almanac* and in his book *Westwood Ha!* he described me as "an amalgam of Groucho Marx and Tallulah Bankhead." Of course, that didn't please me much because I don't care to be an amalgam of anyone, but he also wrote, "She is the wittiest and most engaging performer in many a year and has a touch consistently dextrous." So I forgave him and when we met, I liked him so much that we became friends. He had something almost of the English style about him and he talked in a low-key, droll sort of way that made him nearly as amusing to talk to as he was to read. When S.J. received his Academy Award nomination, he couldn't attend the Hollywood ceremony and so he asked me whether I could go in his place.

"What do I say if you win?" I asked him.

"Oh I won't." He chuckled. "But I'll write you a letter to read out in case I do."

Of course, he did win and I went up to the microphone and read his letter, which began, "I'm unable to be present for a variety of reasons—all of them spicy."

Unfortunately, I can't find a copy of that letter—which is heartbreaking because it was so funny. S.J.'s letter went down so

146

well that the next day the press unanimously raved about it being the highlight of the ceremony. One paper suggested, "Hermione Gingold should get an award for being funnier in 40 seconds than Jerry Lewis was in 102 minutes."

Much later, Arthur Freed told me that it was my Academy Award appearance that made them think of me when they were casting *Gigi*.

I had become well established in America by this time and, thanks to my TV appearances, I was usually recognised as I walked along the New York pavements. The Americans still had trouble pronouncing my name, but all manner of people would make a stab at it and I got quite used to answering to Hermoganie, Herman, Hyman and Hormone.

The Americans were, and still are, extremely friendly and sometimes they do say extraordinary things. Once, I became aware that a fairly elderly couple were following me down Fifth Avenue. I went into Saks, did some shopping, and came out to find that they were still there; tentatively, they approached me and asked, "It is Hermione Gingold, isn't it? You'll never guess how we recognised you—by your face."

I adore shopping and buy lots of lovely clothes, but by the time I get home I usually hate them and give them to the maid. I have the best dressed maid in Manhattan.

I often took my darling dog on television with me. Another variation on the recognition theme was when I was hailed on Madison Avenue by perfect strangers with the words, "We recognised your dog." I love it when people come up and say nice things. I was out shopping with Helen Hayes once when a man came up and said, "Oh, Miss Gingold, thank you for making me laugh so much." Of course, he recognised Helen and smiled with awelike reverence, but I suppose he felt he couldn't say to her, "Thank you for making me cry so much."

I've learned that when people see you on television a lot, they feel they know you personally; it seems to them that you've actually been in their bedrooms, and who knows, perhaps I have.

The Americans are far more forthcoming than the English. Their whole attitude to life seems so different. Once I was out walking; it was cold and I happened to be wearing my mink coat. A man in a bus that had stopped at the lights smiled at me and yelled, "Gee lady, that's a great coat. I'm working extra shifts so I can buy my wife a mink like that." In England they're likely to yell, "What right have you to own a coat like that? Come the revolution, we'll take it off you!"

I love Americans. They're so generous, too. On TV once, I joked that I had a mink everything—except eyelashes. Kind people all over America must have been snip snipping all night, for the next morning hundreds of pairs of mink eyelashes arrived through the post for me.

Nowadays I'm very careful what I say on TV. I never wear or mention fur now or I get complaints from the anti-fur brigade. Besides, when I heard how cruelly they kill animals, it quite sickened me and I decided I could never look an animal in the face if I bought another fur coat. But then I suppose there are quite a few animals who wouldn't want to look me in the face, either. Fortunately, I already have ten fur coats. Also when I'm on TV, I always make a point of announcing that all my jewellery is fake in case any muggers are looking in.

Americans are also extraordinary in what they throw away. Of course, I live in a wealthy part of New York, and although I don't exactly go foraging through people's rubbish bins, I have come across some quite valuable items resting beside bins just awaiting the arrival of the dustmen. I once found a complete set of the *Encyclopaedia Britannica*, and an Empire side table that had obviously been thrown away because it had a small stain on the top. I French polished it and sold it for $250. It's a lovely hobby and who knows what I might find one day? A lot of millionaires started in the junk business.

I get on very well with dustmen. They like me because I always get my housekeeper to package rubbish very neatly. "Oh, yes," they say, "we like your garbage; it's a pleasure to take it away. We always call it Miss Gingold's Gahbbarge!"

I'm also on extremely good terms with firemen; the last fireman I met asked me to autograph his axe.

It was unusually hot one afternoon when I bumped into Gertie Lawrence (she hated being called Gertie). "Isn't it hot!" she exclaimed. "How lucky you are *not* working."

It was unfair as I'd recorded a TV show that morning; nevertheless, I was delighted when as soon as I entered my flat, the maid said Alan Conner, my Hollywood agent, wanted to speak to me urgently.

Alan was a dear but mad agent who kept all his contracts and important letters in the gas oven in his flat. As far as I know, he didn't have an office, but he did get me a lot of films and TV, including *Gigi*—my first Hollywood movie.

On the face of it, he said, my part wasn't large but I would be playing opposite Maurice Chevalier and we would be singing a duet. Alan Conner thought I should do it and I said, "Yes, I'd love to."

I didn't discover exactly why they wanted me for the part until years later when Alan Jay Lerner told me the one thing they wanted my character to avoid was a sentimental performance. "And we knew there was no fear of that from you!" he declared in a way that made me uncertain whether he meant it as an insult or a compliment.

Before I left New York, I had to take singing lessons. Alan Jay Lerner and Frederick Loewe came up to my flat to hear me sing, as they didn't know my range. I was petrified, having no range to speak of, and fearful that when they heard me, they might change their minds. Luckily, they didn't ask me to sing a song, just scales.

It may seem strange but once I was a high coloratura soprano and trained seriously as a singer. Then I got nodules on my vocal chords. One morning it was Mozart and the next, "Old Man River". Actually it happened over several years, but my voice dropped lower and lower. Now I'm a basso profundo and can sing lower than the average man. These days I think it is quite a simple operation to have nodules removed, but fifty years ago it was not without risk and my mother persuaded me not to have it done. I've always regretted it.

I'm sometimes complimented on my voice. James Agate called it "remarkable" and J. C. Trewin said it reminded him of "powdered glass in deep syrup", but I still wish it would trill out the bell song from *Lakmé*. Even now I find it upsetting when I order something on the telephone, and room service says, "Certainly, sir."

Fortunately, my bass growl must have been what Lerner and Loewe wanted, because Alan rang me the next day to tell me to take the earliest possible train to the coast. I packed at once and left with Mr Poodle for Hollywood. Alan Conner met me at the station with his car. I must say the ensuing drive to the Beverly Hills Hotel, where I was going to stay, filled me with dismay. So much was ugly, but when we got nearer to Beverly Hills, it became more as I expected it to be, with lovely houses, palm trees, no billboards, and clean.

We arrived at the hotel, dumped everything into a tiny bed-sittingroom (the bed made into a sofa), which was quite pretty, and then Alan drove me to his flat and produced my contract —which I signed—from the gas oven. Then we went to MGM to meet Arthur Freed, who made me feel very welcome.

150

I also met Sydney Guilaroff, of the hairdressing department, and Cecil Beaton, who was the costume designer. Cecil had taken my photograph several times in London and he was being very grand as usual.

As far as I remember, Alan and I had lunch in the MGM cafeteria, then I met the rest of the cast and we all went upstairs to read the script with Arthur Freed, while André Previn played us the music and Lerner and Loewe sang the songs. I was enchanted by the duet. Of course, mine was a small part, but the duet was far from small.

As production got under way, the first thing I did was to go up to the hairdressing department, where Sydney Guilaroff dyed my hair black, started to style it, then despaired of it, and decided I should wear a wig. Then Cecil Beaton arrived and told Sydney how he wanted my hair done—I hated Cecil's style and thought it made me look awful. Luckily, Sydney thought so too and he and Beaton got into an argument, whereupon Sydney took us both to Freed's office. Sydney said, "Tell Mr Beaton to stay out of the hairdressing department!" Mr Freed obliged and so Sydney and I went back to hairdressing, and Cecil Beaton returned beaten to the costume department, where he went about designing the costumes of the entire cast except mine.

I was very worried about this, and asked Alan Conner to look in my agreement and see whether Cecil could ignore me in this way. It took Alan hours to find my contract, but eventually it turned up in the grill of the gas stove. He said it wasn't even put into print that I was to have a costume, and I was very lucky to get what I got. As so far I had nothing at all, I couldn't agree with him. Eventually, my costumes came from Bermans in London and were definitely secondhand.

Filming *Gigi* was a wonderful experience for me. I found Vincente Minnelli difficult to work for, but that was only because I wasn't used to a director who knew exactly what he wanted. Sometimes it was hard to know what he did want, but he kept on refilming a scene till he got it just as he felt it should be.

All the stars were French—Louis Jourdan, Leslie Caron, and Maurice Chevalier—and all had French accents; my character, Mamita Alvarez, Gigi's grandmother, was French and so I thought it seemed logical for me to have one too, but Minnelli wouldn't even let me have a subtle one.

"They're French," he told me, "you're English." I couldn't quite follow his thinking but I did as I was told.

Isabel Jeans, who was playing Gigi's aunt in the picture, wasn't at all happy, either; we really dreaded the rehearsals before the shooting. She found it quite different from the stage; and as a big star, she wasn't used to being told what sort of inflection to give or to leaving everything to the twenty-five-minute rehearsal before each scene, and then shooting it over and over again. However, she was wonderful in the picture, as indeed everybody was. My duet with Chevalier—"I Remember It Well"—has, I think, become a classic.

We actually filmed the master shot for "I Remember It Well" in only two takes. After the first take, Minnelli said, "You're both making the number too sad—keep it light and cheerful." We sang it again. Of course, Minnelli was absolutely right and he was delighted with the second take.

The most difficult thing for me was recording the songs with the orchestra, only to have to mouth to the recording later when we filmed in the studio.

That procedure came round full circle, for after Chevalier and I filmed our duet, Lerner and Loewe weren't happy with the orchestration. They felt the musical treatment had been too grand and overwhelming for our intimate number. We thought the whole film was complete, but they recalled us both to the studio to resing our duet with a smaller orchestra. This time we watched the film as we sang and had to synchronise our voices to fit the pictures.

Chevalier was wonderful to work with. I found him very warm and giving. He was so used to singing, or mouthing, before the camera that he seemed totally relaxed, which helped to add cohesion and spontaneity to our scene. Chevalier was charm personified, the epitome of the romantic Frenchman; although he could be a little on the stingy side when it came to spending money, he was always a very generous performer.

One thing puzzled me about Chevalier. In the early morning, he always arrived for the six o'clock costume and makeup call looking immaculate. He looked wide awake and smartly dressed, while the rest of us looked as if we had just fallen out of bed.

"Maurice," I asked him, "how do you manage to look as fresh as a daisy at this hour, while everyone else looks as if they're half asleep?"

"Oh, easy," he smiled. "You see 'ermione, I 'ave not yet been to bed."

I still don't know whether he was telling the truth.

I remember one day when we were filming at Trancas Beach on the California coast, pretending it was Trouville on the French coast—very successfully too. With the bathing huts, parasols, and costumes, the scene was a Boudin painting come to life. All was going well until we had to stop filming because the sound technicians were complaining of a terrible clicking noise. It took them two hours to trace the noise to—Chevalier. It turned out that he was wearing a very old set of false teeth. He had some new ones in his dressing room that were sent for and filming was resumed.

I worked only six weeks on *Gigi* and I never left California. The rest of the cast was lucky enough to film in Paris. I still hope one day to get a part in a film that takes months to make, preferably in Egypt, Greece, Turkey, or even China. Of course, I don't think there's much chance of this, but one never knows—and that's why one goes on living after one has reached a certain age.

I went back to New York for the opening of *Gigi*. It was to be played twice a day at the Royale Theatre, and I was invited to the première. I was terribly nervous and spent the first half-hour with my eyes firmly shut, but the audience reaction was so good that I peeked through my false eyelashes and by the time Chevalier and I sang our duet, I was wide-eyed and overjoyed; and I'm glad to say that despite being in a cinema, "I Remember It Well" got terrific applause. Since then I've sung it on television with Jack Paar, Merv Griffin, John Davidson, Ed Wynn, and Lord Boothby. It has also been done by the Muppets, and Dean Martin and Jonathan Winters mouthing it to our gramophone recording; I must say it was hysterically funny.

My next Hollywood film was *Bell, Book, and Candle* and in it I met up again with my old friend Elsa Lanchester. I played a witch; in fact, I was the queen witch. Some people, whose names I do not care to mention, said it was perfect typecasting. Jimmy Stewart and Kim Novak were in it, as well. I played a scene with Ernie Kovacs that took place in a low nightclub. To get a smoky nightclub atmosphere, they kept pumping some evil artificial smoke on to the set, which went straight to my stomach and made me feel very sick. Luckily, the next day was Sunday and I stayed in bed all day. I was living then at the Château Marmont and I was cheered up by darling Elsa, who arrived bearing kippers. This heartened me no end, cleared my chest, and on Monday I was back at work.

Unlike *Gigi*, in *Bell, Book and Candle*, we never rehearsed before shooting and I must say I enjoyed it much more. Also, I loved working with Kim Novak. She was kind, beautiful, and very punctual, although at the time she wasn't having too good a time of it. She was in a relationship with Sammy Davis, which was upsetting Harry Cohn, the head of Columbia. He said, "If it was Harry Belafonte or Poitier I could understand it—but Sammy Davis?!" Kim was the only person I've ever worked with who wrote to me afterward, in her own handwriting, to tell me how nice it was to work with me.

It seemed as though I might be spending a lot of time in Hollywood, so I bought a secondhand Buick that I called Mr Car. I bought Mr Car from a rather fishy salesman. It didn't show much mileage on the clock, but I knew that could be wangled and so I said to the salesman, "I suppose you're going to tell me that dreary old story about the schoolteacher who only used it on Sundays to go to church."

"Oh no, Miss Gingold," he said, "it belonged to someone in the Mafia who seldom used it because he was scared of getting shot."

I was completely won over by that obvious lie and I bought Mr Car; it turned out to be a very good bargain.

Due to a misunderstanding, the Hollywood press rather mocked my lovely car. One day I saw a journalist studying Mr Car; he told me he was doing an article on "Cars of the Stars", so I told him proudly that my car was secondhand and had only cost $400. He asked, "Was it wise to buy a car like this?" I didn't realise it until I read his article later, but he was inferring that I should have a grander car. I thought he meant that perhaps I'd been a little extravagant and I told him confidently, "Oh, I shall try and get my money back by selling it when I leave." When his article came out, it was full of grand Stars all trying to outdo each other by boasting how many thousands of dollars their cars cost and how they'd just throw them away in a few months' time. Then there was a picture of me with Mr Car and my quotes of economy triumphing over ostentation.

I'm afraid this article coupled with another got me a quite unjustified reputation around Hollywood for being a bit of a British eccentric.

The other article was by a profile journalist who interviewed me in my mobile dressing room. I happened to mention that I'd repainted the dressing room furniture myself. He was amazed. "You painted it yourself?"

"Yes—it was cream and it's so much prettier white."

He looked so amazed that I suddenly became worried. "You don't think the studio will be cross do you?"

He laughed and said that in Hollywood if you weren't happy with your dressing room, you contacted your agent, you threatened to sue, you screamed, you walked off the set. The one thing you did not do was buy a paintbrush and paint it yourself. Unfortunately, he printed our conversation word for word. I wasn't trying to be different—I was just ignorant of Hollywood ways.

I also found a Hollywood flat of my own at La Ronda; it was very small but I got out my paintbrush again and painted everything white, had a black-and-white tile floor laid, and filled the flat with Mexican figures. It looked so good that I moved in with Mr Poodle, who I promised wouldn't bark, as dogs really weren't allowed. Mr Car was garaged under the house, which I was told was the oldest house in Hollywood, many famous stars having lived there.

Although I never really cared for Hollywood, I stayed there for quite a while doing a mixture of film and TV parts—*The Jack Benny Show, Hallmark Hall of Fame, Alfred Hitchcock Presents, Fallguy, Banyon, The Girl from UNCLE*, and, of course, the Ed Sullivan, Johnny Carson, and Dick Cavett shows. From the distance of time, they tend to blur into one another, although I have very vivid memories of a bevy of handsome, scantily clad men in *Virtuous Island*, a play by Giraudoux I did with Burgess Meredith.

The only TV show of which I haven't particularly pleasant memories is the *Frank Sinatra Show*. I had a couple of sketches with Frank and quite naturally enough, I thought it might be a good idea to rehearse them. When I asked when we could rehearse the sketches, a man told me, "Frank will send someone down to rehearse with you."

"Don't bother," I replied.

Unprofessional behaviour sickens me and as an actress, it offends me to hear people endlessly asking, "Where are the cue cards?" Why can't people bother to come in and learn their lines? After all, we get paid enough.

Raymond Burr was very professional. He was easy to work with and he loved rehearsing. I was in a two-part *Ironside* episode called "Checkmate: and Murder!" To begin with, I was quite pleased to have what read as a good straight part for once, but on the first day Raymond said, "In this episode, we'd like you to smoke a cigar." Apparently, they'd seen me being silly and smoking a cigar on some chat-show, and I realised at once that I had been booked not because I was an actress but because I was a personality. At first I was a little frightened of Raymond, so I agreed and as the day wore on, I got to like him enormously—so much that I still smoked the cigar. They even got my character to smoke a cigar in bed. During the shooting of the episodes, I must have smoked twenty cigars—it put me off cigars for life—but by that time I'd already decided cigars no longer matched anything I wore.

On *It Takes a Thief*, I had a very strange and rather frightening experience. There I was waltzing around the room with Robert Wagner when suddenly I felt giddy. We stopped dancing and I said, "Bob, I feel most peculiar—the room's going round and round."

"That's strange," said Bob, "the room *is* going round and round."

We were having an earthquake. Bob, I, and the crew knelt down on the floor till the tremors were over. Fortunately, the quake was a little one, no one was hurt, and no damage done, but it was my first and I was quite scared.

The film *The Naked Edge* was a psychological thriller with Michael Wilding and Deborah Kerr. Deborah is perhaps the most "unstarry" star I've ever had the pleasure to work with. She inspires great respect but in a natural and unassuming way.

In the film, Deborah and I were playing two old friends. Discussing the relationship of our characters—where we'd met and what situations we'd shared together—was great fun. Deborah has a very amusing sense of humour and I found her delightful to play against.

The Naked Edge was also the last film Gary Cooper ever made. He was already seriously ill and died soon after, but he never once grumbled or asked to be let off early. The only clue to his illness was that his wife and daughter came with him every day and stayed in the studio until he left. They must have known and didn't want to leave him for a minute in case anything happened.

It was during the filming of *The Naked Edge* that I took up the hobby of needlepoint tapestry. I couldn't bear doing nothing during the long waits in between takes; it was hard to concentrate on reading a book, so I began to sew. It was wonderfully relaxing therapy. My needlepoint became really rather proficient and I went on to complete a large tapestry of the flower emblems of each of the twenty-four American states I'd visited at that time. This was displayed in the Hallmark gallery in New York and was eventually auctioned for charity. I forget how much money it made, but it was a considerable amount.

I am also a founding member of "The Golden Thimble Club". There were three other founding members: Celeste Holm, June Havoc, and her sister, Gypsy Rose Lee, who could put a stitch on surprisingly well. We used to do our needlework as we sat talking *Girl Talk* on TV, and we four became adept at putting the needle in.

Some people are surprised that I do needlepoint—they think I spend all my time counting my money and cleaning my jewels.

Another big musical picture I did was *The Music Man* with Robert Preston and Shirley Jones. I played the mayor's wife,

Eulalie Shinn, and I had to sing again. I found one song particularly difficult; it was called "Pick a Little Talk a Little, Chirp Chirp Chirp, Talk a Lot, Pick a Little More"—and that was just the title. I didn't have time to learn the lyrics properly, but I did have time to learn the word *Balzac*, which I boomed out loud and clear at the end of each verse. It got a huge laugh both on the set and at the premiere, and *Balzac* became quite a catchword around the studio.

Also, I began to do a lot more chat shows. Some chat-show hosts are good, but I have to say that the majority of interviewers are rather stupid people and the questions they ask are so repetitive that you can develop stock answers for them. Strangely enough, I seemed to go over best when confronted with an unusual or totally unexpected question. For example, when I was asked in all seriousness, "Why did the English soldiers burn Joan of Arc?" I answered, "Because they were cold." Well, if you ask a silly question, you get a silly answer.

On another chat show, I was asked, "What do you think of Elsa Maxwell?" I answered, "She's just another pretty face."

They tell me this reply of mine has become popular to describe anyone who is over sixty and rather ugly and fat.

This became the start of what appeared to be a feud between Elsa and me. Actually, we were really friends all through it, although certainly not bosom friends. Miss Maxwell would have had an overwhelming advantage if we were.

When Elsa published her book, she asked me to make a speech at her literary lunch, which shows you what we thought of one another. Her book was called *I Married the World*, and I got up and said, "I hope you'll both be very happy."

Years ago, in England, I was asked, "How did you find New York?" It seemed such an inane question that I replied, "I didn't have to, the ship was going there anyway." It's been used to death since, but I believe I was the first to say it.

I remember doing one chat show that was peopled by very dull guests. They were all taking themselves seriously and discussing the first words they'd uttered—real gems like "mama", "dad-dad", and "bowwow". I felt it was my duty to liven things up and put them in their place, so when they asked, "Hermione what were your first words?" I told them I didn't speak until I was eighteen because I couldn't think of anything interesting to say.

The most appalling interview I ever endured was in England in 1965 on television. The host began by introducing me as an "unlovely middle-aged eccentric", which wasn't, I felt, an auspicious beginning. Further ungallantries followed, such as, "What is there left in life for a veteran actress like you?"

That was nothing compared with what came next. Eartha Kitt, the American singer and actress, joined us. She looked stunning and walked in wearing white fox and diamonds, looking every inch the star she was. The host looked her up and down and said, "Well this makes a change from picking cotton!"

The rudeness and insensitivity of his remark astounded me; I felt so embarrassed. The host was British and so was I, and his rudeness to a visiting American made me ashamed. I nearly got up and walked out of the interview, but never being one to take the coward's way, I stayed and Eartha and I soon graciously put him in his place. I am amazed to learn that this rude and incompetent man is still working for the BBC. In Lord Reith's day, he would have been dismissed or banned from reading the epilogue for at least a month.

Over the years, I have developed a rather piercing look for squashing interviewers who get above themselves. I just give them one of my "shrivellers," as I call them. I don't usually have any trouble after that.

160

Magazine and newspaper interviewers aren't so easy to handle. On TV the viewers can make up their own minds whether they like you or not, but in a one-to-one confrontation with a journalist, you have no choice but to trust his or her integrity. On the whole, the press have always been very generous to me. I've also got on well with Louella Parsons, Hedda Hopper, and Radie Harris, three of the most powerful gossip columnists in America, but through experience I've learned to be very wary of lesser journalists—particularly women.

I once had an interview with one over lunch at the Plaza Hotel in New York. The woman interviewer began by asking me how old I was. I loathe the continual obsession with age—you're as young or old as you feel. I told her, "I'm so old that when my lawyer sent for my documents from England, they arrived written on parchment." That answer didn't satisfy her and she asked me to be more precise. I found her persistence impertinent and I suggested she look up my age in *Who's Who* or *Who's Who in the British Theatre*, or the American equivalents. I thought she'd enjoy that little job, as she'd find a different date in each of them. She didn't drop her line of questioning, so I asked her how old *she* was; she didn't like that a bit. I said, "Why should I tell you my age if you won't tell me yours, and why should you think actresses are impervious to people asking them their age?"

We got over that hurdle and the interview seemed to progress quite well. She didn't ask me any more personal or pertinent questions, and we parted in a friendly way. I thanked her and she said she'd send me a copy of what she'd written. When it came, I was amazed. She made me out to be a most terrible person, a vicious, debauched old harridan, and she claimed I'd insulted her. Fortunately, the article was never published in New York, but at the time it was upsetting and there wasn't a thing I could do about it.

Rona Barrett was unfair to me, too. When I first went to Hollywood, MGM said the spaces between my teeth were too big and I'd have to get them capped. It's true that I have large spaces. My teeth are tiny because I never grew my second ones; but although my teeth are small, they're very good. In fact, I've never had a single filling. I didn't want to part with any portion of my teeth to get permanent caps, so they gave me four caps that just slip on; they look good but you can't eat in them. I was filming at United Artists and when I had to eat my lunch in the canteen, I slipped off my caps, put them in an ashtray, and forgot them. I went back to find them and when someone asked me what I was looking for, I said, apparently quite loudly, "I'm looking for my caps."

In the paper the next day, Rona Barrett announced, "Hermione Gingold lost her complete set of false teeth."

With these few exceptions, the press have been, for the most part, very fair to me. Over the years, a similar pattern of questions seems to have emerged and I usually try to give each profile reporter an original and fresh answer. For example, the following question has been asked of me a dozen times, first by a journalist from *The New Yorker* (who should have known better) and on later occasions by other rags. Here are three of my replies to the question "Do Englishmen make good lovers?"

"The trouble with most of them is inbreeding and too many brussels sprouts."

"Yes, they are divine."

"Only as long as they're millionaires. All men should be millionaires—it's best for them. Behind every successful man is a bad woman."

All three answers were true according to how I felt at the time. In any case it's such a silly question—how can you generalise about a subject as complex as men? A good journalist often researches through past press clippings and hence a headline emerges such as, MISS G. CHANGES HER MIND ABOUT ENGLISH-MEN. Well, I haven't changed my mind at all; I never made it up in the first place.

On another occasion an American journalist wanted me to explain why my book was called *The World is Square*.

"Do you mean square in the beatnik or Jazz sense?" he asked me.

162

"Heavens no," I told him, "I don't mean square in your American sense. I mean it literally. I am simply saying that the world is not round, as everyone since Columbus has insisted, but that it is square."

"You believe the world isn't round?" he asked incredulously.

"Oh no, that's not the point of it at all. I merely want to argue. If you agree with everything, you learn nothing."

"So your book is a sort of geographical thesis?"

I gave up then. Some things you just can't explain.

The silliest press interview I ever gave began with my being asked, "What are your vital statistics?" I answered, "At my age, everything is vital—everything."

"Oh, I see," said the inexperienced interviewer, "well might I ask you how do American men strike you?"

"They never strike me—they're very kind to me."

The interviewer looked embarrassed. "I'm sorry I didn't phrase that too well. I do hope you won't think too badly of the *Chattanooga Home Journal*."

"I promise I won't think of it at all."

I didn't like living in Hollywood; it's a plastic place. Whenever I'm there, I feel part of me is missing—I'm not sure which part (no letters please). I took the money and ran back to New York, which I love.

I opened there at the Alvin Theatre in a new musical version of *Pride and Prejudice* with Farley Granger and Polly Bergen. The show was called *First Impressions*. It's not generally known, but Jane Austen wanted to call her novel *First Impressions*, but another author beat her to it, so she settled for *Pride and Prejudice*—quite a catchy title.

I played Mrs Bennet and had two good solo numbers in the show: "A House in Town", where I'm imagining all the magnificent things that I'll have when I marry my daughters off to wealthy men; and "Five Daughters", where I'm bemoaning the fact that no one seems to want to marry them:

> *Daughters help a home to thrive*
> *and I've got five!*

Kenneth Tynan said of my performance: "As played by Hermione Gingold, Mrs Bennet is no longer the vague, fussy, provincial matchmaker of Jane Austen's imagination but a bubbling dragoness fully capable of withering her husband with a single fire-darting glare. Needless to say most of what Miss Gingold does is strangely hilarious. No actor commands a more purposeful leer, and in nobody's mouth do vowels more acidly curdle." I think he was trying to be nice.

I'm sorry *First Impressions* wasn't a hit. Some of the music was good, but Jane Austen got lost. I'm sorry to say it, but I think Abe Burrows was the wrong director for that show. We were all playing on different levels and I think it could have been a success if we'd had an English director.

My new penthouse flat in Manhattan had three roof terraces. At one stage, I grew all my own vegetables on them. You wouldn't think slugs could find their way up to the seventeenth floor but they did, and I found the most enormous hairy green caterpillars on my tomatoes. I didn't like to squash them, so

I dropped them over the parapet and hoped they'd turn into butterflies on the way down.

I fitted my flat with the things I love—my blue Bristol glass, my early naive paintings of children, my zebra rugs, and several blackamoor statues of Nubian slaves bearing lanterns and aspidistras. I've also a beautiful Georgian stool in the shape of an Egyptian cat with a long tail, and a life-sized wooden monkey holding a tray. Some people find the monkey bizarre, but I love the exotic and extraordinary. When my friends look round, they frequently say, "Oh yes, the flat is very you." I'm never sure how to take that.

My style is a combination of Georgian, Regency, Biedermeier, and Victorian—a real mishmash, which I suppose is just like me. For years Noël Coward had a pied-à-terre in the same building; because he wasn't there very often, he only partly furnished his flat. One day Noël rang and said Ed Murrow wanted to interview him on *Person to Person* and, as they always filmed their guests in their own flat, could I lend him some of my furniture to augment his own. I had to tell him, "Sorry, Noël, but my furniture has already been on *Person to Person*." So he had to borrow his furniture elsewhere.

In its own way, my flat has become quite famous. It has been featured in *House and Gardens* and *House Beautiful* and has been subjected to that quaint American custom of "tours"—where members of the public give money to charity for the privilege of peering under your bed or peeping into your closets. In England people only tour round palatial stately homes, so when my English chums hear people tour my flat, they think it must be wonderfully grand and they start trying to borrow money. It isn't grand but it is pretty, I think.

I was away when one of these tours came round, so my maid supervised it. One visitor was in my bedroom, which is in white wicker and has a brass bed; the bed isn't overly large, perfect for one and cosy for two if the gentleman doesn't stay too long. The tour visitor looked aghast at my bed and exclaimed, "It's a very small bed—where does Miss Gingold's husband sleep?"

My maid answered, "In England." I couldn't have put it better myself.

When I was once asked, "Miss Gingold is your husband living?" I said, "It's a matter of opinion."

My final gesture of commitment to America was when I shipped my white grand piano from England. I have never taken out American citizenship and I remain to this day what is known as a "resident alien". Of course, I realise this prohibits me from ever becoming President, but I've resigned myself to that. I don't get a vote either, but I don't think that will change the course of history. I love America and it's been very good to me, but part of me is British and always will be.

I adore it when my English actor friends come to visit me in New York. Peter Bull was one of my favourites and when he was playing in *Luther* over here, we discovered a wonderful British-style olde-tea-shoppe restaurant to dine at. It was run by an ancient little English lady who was an excellent cook but a very poor typist. We used to have such fun ordering.

"We'll start with the Gropefruit, followed by the Beef and twe veg, then we'll have Rhubarb pee for dessert."

Another of my favourite British guests is Lord Snowdon, whom I knew as Antony Armstrong-Jones. He used to be married to the Queen's sister, Princess Margaret, but it didn't work out. I loved showing him round New York, but when he asked me, "Why is all that steam gushing out of the manholes?" I had to admit, "I don't know darling; it's either the Indians down below smoking in their reservations or they're trying to elect a new Pope."

I also love it when my American friends, about to visit England, seek me out as an authority on how to behave on the other side of the Atlantic. Of course, I adore giving advice and give it at the drop of a dollar. I tell them that the necessary clothing for England is a simple morning coat with a pearl-grey cravat, a top hat, and a properly furled umbrella. This attire should be adequate for most occasions. My other hot tip for England concerns royalty: don't just drop in at Buckingham Palace—phone first.

No sooner had I got my New York flat perfect than *First Impressions* closed and I set off again to tour the States in another revue. It was called *From A to Z*, but the show never made it to Broadway and I've never really understood why. The show had a strong cast and some wonderful material, including a number by Jerry Herman called "Best Gold" and two sketches by Woody Allen. One was "Psychological Warfare" and another, "Hit Parade", which I performed with Alvin Epstein, was extremely funny.

I didn't realise at the time, but *From A to Z* was the last real stage revue I was ever to do. Of course, I went on to do lots of comedy numbers and sketches on TV, but intimate revue as a popular entertainment form seems to have disappeared completely both in America and England. It had a final flare up in the sixties with Jonathan Miller's *Beyond the Fringe* and Alan Bennett and "The Establishment", but that was short-lived.

The only explanation I can think of is that the lure of television and its ever-consuming need for comedy material has stolen all the best writers and performers who otherwise would have done stage revues. Perhaps an evening's TV viewing—a comedy show followed by a devastating news bulletin or current-affairs programme—is too similar to a stage revue, for the best revue format was always one that interspersed high comedy with serious numbers and penetrating satire on topical events.

Yet I find so much of television's so-called "comedy" banal, crude, or repetitive. A large demand to fill air time must, I suppose, inevitably encourage mediocrity. It's so easy to portray President Reagan as a dribbling idiot, but that's not clever, merely rude. I also think there is far too much violence on TV; it distorts the value of life. I heard a true story recently of a mother who told her little boy, "Darling, I'm very sorry to tell you this but Granny has died and gone to heaven."

"Who shot her?" the child asked.

I was sorry *From A to Z* wasn't a success, but I was well established in America by now and I had no shortage of offers of work. I ended up in Hollywood filming again.

In *I'd Rather Be Rich* for Universal, I was teamed again with Chevalier, he playing a wealthy invalid and I his hospital nurse. To say it lacked the magic of *Gigi* is an understatement.

I rented a beautiful house at Malibu. It wasn't very well furnished but had the advantage of being right on the beach.

At this time, my beloved Mr Poodle died. I couldn't bring myself to get another poodle and instead got two Yorkshire terriers, Mr Pudding (well, he was from Yorkshire) and Messy Missey (well, she was at first).

They were dear dogs. Mr Pudding was a great character and his only fault was that he aspired to become the Capability Brown of the canine world. He believed he had green paws and he would rush out on to my terrace, jump on to my flower beds, and dig up the seeds to see how they were getting on. Messy Missey was a darling but proved very difficult to train; she was beautifully house-trained but I wanted her garden-trained. I eventually managed to newspaper-train her and it was particularly gratifying to me to get her to pee on any bad press notices I got. She grew accustomed to peeing on *The New York Times* and when *The New York Times* went on strike, I tried to persuade her to relieve dame nature on the *Village Voice* but she absolutely refused. She was a very classy dog. My Yorkies were tiny; their combined weight was only five pounds. Once someone sent me a packet of Venus's flytrap seeds, but I never planted them in case they grew and ate the dogs.

Among other things, I recorded a Walt Disney animated film called *Gay Purree* in which Judy Garland and I played the voices of pussy cats. As *Gay Purree* was a feature cartoon, we didn't appear in the film but just provided the dialogue. The sound director thought Judy and I wouldn't be able to purr and he brought a "purring machine" into the studio, but we said we didn't need a machine and we did all our own purring. It's a strange experience to dub a cartoon. I did a subsequent one called *Tubby the Tuba* where the cartoon character I was playing was actually drawn to resemble me physically. When I watched it, I kept thinking, Oh, I wouldn't do that movement on that line. I had to keep reminding myself that it wasn't me at all, but an animated drawing.

Judy Garland was delightful to work with and I adored her. She had a fragile, nervous quality—one moment giggling and joking and the next moment seeming close to tears. Then she'd laugh again, and as soon as the recording tape started rolling, she'd concentrate with all the intensity of the true professional she was, only to collapse in giggles again when "cut" was called.

I felt sorry for Judy. For all her fame, I felt she didn't have a friend in the world. I believe she was also short of money. I saw her later in New York standing outside a building on Fifty-seventh Street. She was being turned out of her flat and having a row with a man who was holding her clothes and was refusing to hand them to her until she paid him some back rent. I felt she might be embarrassed to think I'd seen this episode, so to my everlasting shame, I crossed over to the other side—actually I was in a taxi, but it still haunts me whether I should have stopped or not. I felt so sorry for her—she seemed completely alone.

When I finished *Gay Purree*, Beaudoin, to whom I'd said good-bye in London, suddenly rang to say he was in Hollywood. We went out to tea to celebrate his arrival.

We were just on our second cup when a talent scout from

Columbia Studios came over to our table and introduced himself. I began to flutter my false eyelashes madly and nearly swallowed the tea bag when he asked, not me, but Beaudoin whether he'd like to be in a new costume drama that his studio was making. Beaudoin laughed and said he wasn't interested in being in pictures. I was sure hearing Beaudoin's heavy French Canadian accent would make the talent scout regret his offer, but he seemed keener than ever. Beaudoin explained politely that he was training to be a pilot, as flying was his idea of living.

"Or dying," said the scout, adding, "If you change your mind, phone me," and he gave Beaudoin his card.

We called for our bill and left in my car for Malibu, where we lived for some weeks before parting. Beaudoin never rang the man from Columbia.

My affair with Beaudoin has been on and off for years. We later got engaged, but in all honesty it was only a half-hearted engagement because I decided by then that I really didn't believe in marriage. I was also becoming more and more used to suiting myself and living on my own, which does make one astonishingly selfish. I began to think that even if I met a man who was the type to let his life revolve around mine, he would only succeed in making me feel giddy; so I decided that if marriage did seriously ever rear its ugly head again, I'd let the gentleman in question off gently by telling him, "I refuse to make you miserable." My married friends sometimes say how nice it would be for me to have a husband's shoulder to cry on, but I have decided that even if I do marry again, there'd be no guarantee my husband's shoulder would be available. As yet, I have not found it difficult to find a shoulder at times of dire distress.

J D. is a mystery character I feel no unrespectable memoir should be without. In order to make him even more mysterious, I shall allude to him only by his initials. It's not for nothing that I read Agatha Christie. Although knowing J.D., I don't suppose for a minute they were his real initials. J.D. was always dressed smartly but not overdressed. I'm not sure that his perfume of Royal Hyacinth wasn't a bit much, but I put up with it because J.D. was fun. Whenever I was bored with a life of pomp and circumstance, a phone call to J.D. was a guaranteed antidote.

I met him first in London. It was a beautifully sunny morning and I thought I would walk through the park and call on my friend Rodney Ackland at his rooms in Albany. Rodney's new play had just opened and although it was about twelve o'clock, he was still in his dressing gown pasting up newspaper clippings. The critics had been very kind about his play and Rodney had reason to believe it would run a long time.

The house phone rang.

"Two gentlemen down below," a voice told Rodney. "One gentleman says he's Prince Philip—the other gentleman just says he's a friend."

"Let them both up," said Rodney, hiding the clippings book under a cushion.

A few minutes later, the door opened and Prince Philip came in, followed by a man who I later learnt was J.D.

"Good morning Your Highness and friend," I said, curtsying low. J.D. started explaining to Rodney, "I came over for a bit of a holiday and so far I've spent the whole time playing bridge with Winston Churchill." Rodney said something about that not being much fun.

"But Winston is a very good bridge player," said J.D. defensively. As we seemed to be heading for a long dissertation on bridge playing for fun, I left, saying, as I always do, "Show me a man who plays bridge for fun and I'll show you a man who never gets asked to play bridge anywhere."

I met up again with J.D. in New York. He loved the theatre and in his large flat he was always giving lavish dinner parties for never less than twenty people. The food would be cooked beautifully and served to handsome men and women whom I'd never met before and who vanished the next day leaving no traces.

J.D. had studied for the law but didn't practise it. In fact, he seemed to have no business at all, except to enjoy himself. Sadly, my friends didn't like J.D. Some begged me not to be seen with him in public, and others went so far as to say the police were looking for him. It seemed absurd to me—he'd lived for a long time at the same Park Avenue address and had the same staff for years. I was certain the police knew where to find him if they wanted him, which I doubted, and besides I liked him.

I went to London to make a film called *Promise Her Anything* with Warren Beatty and Leslie Caron. The character I was playing was an ex-vaudeville girl who keeps a boarding house; one of her boarders makes blue films and can't pay the rent. Instead of paying up, he offers to make a film about her. She wore two live doves on top of her head at all times. (Actually, they were pigeons pretending to be doves—all pigeons are character actors.) J.D. was in London too, which proved fortunate.

One dreadful night, we were filming some scenes a little way out of the city. It was three in the morning and pouring with rain when I slipped in a puddle and sprained my ankle. I was sent in a studio car to St George's Hospital, where I had to wait more than an hour. I watched with fascination as a charlady came in carrying a bucket of what seemed to be liquid mud and promptly washed the floor with it, making it dirtier than it already was. I was then taken to lie in a bloodstained bed while I waited for a woman doctor to bicycle up from some place in the country. She arrived and told me I'd have to rest my leg for a week or two. I explained my position to her but she stuck to her guns.

"You won't be able to walk," she said, "or stand on your leg.

172

You must stay in bed." As I had no maid and no stand-in, it all seemed like an impossible dream, if not a nightmare. . . .

The studio car took me back to my flat. The driver carried me upstairs, dumped me on the sofa, and left. Then the phone rang. Luckily, the phone was on a table near the sofa, so I managed to answer it. It was J.D.

I don't know how he found out where I was staying, but I've never been more pleased to hear his voice. I told him what had happened and how miserable I was, and hurt, and that there was nothing to eat in the house. He said "Don't move"—as if I could—and in no time at all, he arrived with a waiter from the Dorchester who served lobster salad, Brie, and champagne.

"And I've arranged for you to see a marvellous doctor," J.D. announced. "The most marvellous in all England. This man does footballers and mountain climbers and he'll have you back at work in no time. I'll come and collect you at ten-thirty in the morning." The next morning he did pick me up at ten-thirty, and by eleven o'clock I sat with my foot encased in hot mud, and felt much better. By twelve o'clock, I was able to walk a little. I phoned the studio and told them I could stand but not walk.

"That'll be all right," they said, and I was again back at work as Warren Beatty's landlady with the two live pigeons on my head. I rang the Dorchester to thank J.D. but he'd left.

When I arrived again in New York, a very nice-looking boy thrust a paper in my hands, commanding me to appear in a New York court where I would be questioned about J.D.'s character. I was amazed. My first thought was to flee the country. Then I thought of all the nice things J.D. had done for me. I decided this was the one time I could do something for him. So I put on my best hat and went to the courtrooms, which were in a huge building downtown.

I was hustled in by two enormous policemen, and there at the other end of the small courtroom was J.D. I waved to him and he waved back. Then it became like a film script.

When they called my name and I walked to the witness box, the jury broke into a round of applause. I was put into the witness box, given a Bible, and asked to swear to tell the whole truth and nothing but the truth, which is awkward for me because I can't remember from one day to the next what's happened. Still, I thought I might have a try at it.

"Miss Gingold," the magistrate said, "how did you come to meet this man?"

"I met this man," I replied truthfully, "when he visited Albany with Prince Philip."

That, of course, was a blow in my friend's favour, and the magistrate took some time to recover. Then he said, "And what was he doing in London?"

"He was just enjoying himself, you know, playing bridge with Winston Churchill—for fun," I answered.

"Enough," said the magistrate, "I've heard quite enough about his character, thank you."

"Oh dear," I said to him, "I've just begun to enjoy myself."

"Me too," said the magistrate—and the jury also called out that they were enjoying it, and there were cries of "more" and "encore". But the magistrate said, "I'm very sorry but I've heard all I wanted to know—Miss Gingold may go."

I was then ushered out of the building and sent home. I haven't seen J.D. since, and that was years ago. But if he reads this book, I wish he would phone me, as half the fun has gone out of my life.

B ack in New York, life was busy with more TV, films and tours—this time in the play *Abracadabra*, an insane, wildly funny, brilliant play that I wrote myself. My play was taken from the original Russian—and I had trouble getting it away from him. Actually, it was about a crazy husband and wife team of theatrical illusionists who kept making each other disappear.

I thought it had some very funny lines and situations.

"What's a picture of Al Jolson doing in your scrapbook?"

"That's not Al Jolson—that's me as Othello."

And when a guest came to tea: "He knows nothing about women—well what do you expect? He's a sociologist."

Of course, I wrote a marvellous part for myself—why else would I write a play? But its tour wasn't a success and I was forced to tell myself, Hermione, don't look now but your show's slipping.

On Broadway I joined the cast of *Milk and Honey*, taking over the part of Clara Weiss from Molly Picon, and it was during the run of *Milk and Honey* that I was burgled for the fifth time. I loved my roof terraces but it seemed the robbers did too, for this is how they kept breaking in.

They took all my jewellery, including a very heavy gold charm bracelet that I'd been presented with in Hollywood for undergoing my *This Is Your Life* ordeal. Each charm had been specially made to represent a different episode in my life. I remember there was a globe for *Around the World in Eighty Days*, two tiny cribs to represent the births of my children, and a ball and chain for my marriages. It was irreplaceable and I was very upset at it being taken.

The final straw came when the thieves showed extreme bad taste by taking everything they could lay their hands on, except my fur coats. These they looked over and rejected, throwing them into a heap on the bed. It was time to move.

I'd grown fond of East Fifty-fourth Street and stayed in the same building, but I moved down to a lower flat. It has a

175

marvellous thirty-eight-foot sitting room, no free-for-all roof terraces, and it's been my home ever since.

In the sixties, I began a new career as a concert artist. I was invited to do *Façade*, reciting Edith Sitwell's verses to Sir William Walton's music. It's beautiful music and although the verses are partly nonsensical, they are very amusing and make wonderful word patterns:

> *The stars in their apiaries*
> *Sylphs in their aviaries*

blending with the music to create changes of moods and atmosphere. My favourite was "Black Mrs Behemoth" who "gave way to wrath and the wildest malice". Some of the verses have to be delivered at a very fast tempo and all require strict and precise musical discipline. I'm no musician and I worked hard to get them right. I performed *Façade* with orchestras all over America and became quite well-known on the concert circuit.

In 1965 I received an offer from England that I couldn't refuse. It was to appear at the Royal Albert Hall in their summer season of Promenade Concerts. I was to perform *Façade* with Russell Oberlin and the Melos Ensemble, with Sir William himself conducting.

I was nervous about performing with Sir William; after all, he'd written the piece and conducted its first performance in 1922, with Sitwell hidden behind a screen declaiming her own verses through a megaphone. She was concealed as the work was considered radical in those days; they pretended it was to make the speaker's voice disembodied, but in reality they were frightened people would throw things—and they did.

For the Albert Hall concert, I was not concealed, but I did, I believe, use a microphone and no one threw anything except flowers. In fact, the audience went mad, but in the right way. All the young promenaders stood in the floor of the hall following their scores, and never in my life have I had such a reception. It was a magical evening.

I wore a long peacock-blue tartan dress and I got my gloves and shoes dyed to the exact shade of the dress—and, vanity bowing to accuracy, I wore my glasses. They, too, had peacock-blue frames. Being tartan the dress seemed particularly suitable for the "Scotch Rhapsody" poem. When I declaimed the line, "Venus wore tarlatan", it got a huge laugh.

Sir William was an absolute lamb. He had marvellous piercing blue eyes and in rehearsal he'd twinkle at me.

"Hermione dear, I think if you look carefully, you'll see it says 'Banditto' in your score."

"What did I say?"

"Bandetto!"

"Sorry. I'll underline it."

The last performance I'd given had been at the New York City Hall and I'd taken certain liberties, but I hadn't Sir William then. He was rather amused at rehearsals because he was so busy conducting the orchestra that he kept forgetting to give me the downbeat for the entry of the verses. I came in anyway but reminded him that he hadn't brought me in.

"But Hermione, I don't need to, you keep coming in dead on the right beat."

I said, "I know, but I'd feel much happier if you brought me in."

He chuckled and tried to remember.

The evening was marred for me slightly as, during rehearsals, I developed laryngitis and on the evening of the concert, I had a temperature of 103°. But nothing would have kept me from the Albert Hall, and though I thought I wasn't at my best, Sir William gave me hearty congratulations and I felt I had his seal of approval.

I think I must have been all right, as if you don't keep in strict time, you don't come to the end when the orchestra does, and I always did.

On this trip, the BBC gave me my own TV series, a mishmash of songs, sketches, and guests, which I called *Pure Gingold*.

I also recorded a TV special for Alan Melville. It was a nostalgia programme called *Before the Fringe* and in it I was briefly reunited with Hermione Baddeley to recreate some of our early revue sketches. Baddeley was up to her usual tricks. We rehearsed in a dingy hall in Shepherds Bush and I arrived at the appointed hour with the sketches we were to do relearnt. Baddeley arrived two hours late and knew not a word. I hate performing old out-of-date material and I only agreed to do the programme because Alan persuaded me that it was valuable for the BBC archives to have a film of Baddeley and me working together. I've since heard that some tidy soul at the BBC wiped all the tapes so they could be reused.

It was around this time that old Anney entered my life. I say old Anney, for she has a wit and wisdom way beyond her years, but she was a fat, revoltingly stagestruck twelve-year-old when I first encountered her. She wormed her way into my life with a persistence that makes one wonder how Britain lost the Empire. She gave me no choice but to notice her, for wherever I went in England, there she was. With a spy network that would have made the CIA envious, she seemed to know my every move. She'd play truant from school and as if by magic would appear from behind a trunk at Victoria Station, peer through rehearsal studio windows, and once she arrived at Southampton docks in her school uniform with a cake iced "from your little ray of sunshine". By chance, this cake presentation was televised and I felt guilty when she gleefully told me that her headmistress had seen it and she'd been expelled from school. Anne is one of life's true eccentrics, and that's from one who knows a true eccentric when she sees one. I soon grew to love her dearly and she became my "adopted daughter".

Anney grew up and became my dearest, in fact my only, woman friend. She's now slim, very beautiful, and extremely talented. Under her maiden name of Anne Clements, she's had considerable success as an actress. In the seventies, she fell passionately in love with a Conservative member of Parliament. They married and Anne is now Lady Eyre. In 1979 she gave birth to my god-daughter and named her Hermione—poor child! It's only Anney who would choose a godmother who is not religious, hates children, and lives three thousand miles away.

I returned to Broadway in Arthur Kopit's strange play, *Oh Dad, Poor Dad, Mamma's Hung You in the Closet, and I'm Feelin' So Sad*. I took over the part of Madame Rosepettle from Jo Van Fleet and toured the States with the show. The tour was a great success and I reopened it on Broadway again at the Morosco Theatre to rave notices. I loved the play. It's a curious but brilliant black comedy about a lady who travels the world with a collection of weird and wonderful creatures, such as a stuttering son, carnivorous Venus flytrap plants, cat-eating piranha fish (Siamese kittens preferred), and her dead husband stuffed in a bedroom closet. She didn't think much of him: "he was as ugly as a humid day—and just about as wet." Arthur simply describes the play as "A pseudo classical tragi-farce in a bastard French tradition."

Madame Rosepettle is a demanding role. She hardly leaves the stage for the entire play and has a twenty-minute monologue in the third act, and on Broadway we performed the play without intermissions so as not to destroy the atmosphere. I adored playing the part of Madame Rosepettle. Of all the straight dramatic roles I've ever played, this part is unquestionably the one I like most. Jerome Robbins, who directed it, was wonderful to work with and is probably my favourite director of straight drama.

Later I returned to London to play Madame Rosepettle at the Piccadilly Theatre. I hadn't appeared on the West End stage for fifteen years and my opening word, "Fools!", got quite an ovation. I'm afraid the play was too American for British audiences and was not a success. Some of my reviews were good, and Philip Hope Wallace wrote in the *Guardian* that my return to the West End "was a cause for cheering". That was nice, but he went on to say, "Strutting like a parody of every tragedy queen, male or female, since time began, she was in splendid relishing form—her lips drawn back over fangs and her voice swooping campingly through a whole two octaves of sneer."

This was just the sort of review I hate. I wanted to be taken seriously as an actress in a straight dramatic role. True, Madame Rosepettle was a matriarchal monster, but I tried to make her a real rounded person with a sympathetic touch of humanity. Unfortunately, I felt the critics and the audience went to the play with preconceived expectations of me "camping it up" in some sort of elongated revue sketch. It made me realise it would be hard for me ever to be accepted as a classical dramatic actress.

James Agate once said he'd love to see me playing Lady Macbeth or Hedda Gabler, and I knew time and the National Theatre were passing me by. However, I love a challenge and I still cherish hopes of being offered the lead in a production of *Hamlet* one day. I may not be living in fantasy; after all, Sarah Bernhardt was seventy-five when she played it—and she had a wooden leg.

The sixties was the era when 50,000 hippies trampled the grass in Central Park and asked, "Where have all the flowers gone?"

England was going through a curious phase, too. When I did *Oh, Dad, Poor Dad* in London, it was 1965. For the part of my son in the play, we eventually cast Murray Melvin, but we auditioned forty actors; they all seemed to talk with Liverpool accents, including one boy who'd been to Eton and RADA. He was broad scouse and I asked him why he adopted such an accent?

"I must be with it" was all the answer he could give. If that's what being "with it" is all about, I'd rather be without it.

The hippie conformity of the sixties seemed to be men with unkempt shoulder-length hair, ethnic beads, and no personal hygiene. Not entirely true—I did see a man washing in one of the fountains in Trafalgar Square. It was then that I knew that loving London as I do, I could never live there again.

Bond Street was full of thick-thighed women wearing mini-skirts and eating ice creams. It was so different from the smart Bond Street of my childhood, when my mother had chastised me, saying, "I'm afraid you cannot come down Bond Street with us today, Hermione, as you have a small spot on one of your white gloves."

In Piccadilly Circus, I was horrified to see Eros surrounded by "Islanders" with rucksacks who seemed to have set up permanent camp. It appeared that all the buildings I loved most were being pulled down and being replaced with chopped-off office blocks that seemed totally out of place. There were also supermarkets and hamburger joints; it seemed they were well on the way to making my dear old London a shoddy imitation of New York and a home away from home for the American tourists, who I hope, unlike me, won't find it too expensive.

I also managed to make some family visits. My sister Margaret had given up a career as a portrait artist to marry a naval commander and live in Southsea, Hampshire. My eldest son Leslie had become a civil engineer and had moved to Scotland,

and Stephen was running his theatre in Scarborough. I'm so glad I visited him there, because it was the last time I was to see him before he died.

It was lovely to see old friends and family, but seeing London going through her swinging-sixties phase upset me dreadfully and I couldn't wait to get back to New York.

As usual, I didn't stay in New York for long because the Hollywood dollars lured me once again into more TV and films, such as *Munsters Go Home!* in which Terry-Thomas and I played brother and sister.

One of my favourite TV shows was *The Special London Bridge Special*. The show starred Tom Jones, Kirk Douglas, Charlton Heston, Elliott Gould, Engelbert Humperdink, the Carpenters, Rudolf Nureyev, Merle Park, Terry-Thomas, Chief Dan George, and me. Pity they couldn't have got a stronger cast.

At first I thought it was a joke when I heard an American had bought London Bridge from the Corporation of the City of London. But no, they paid millions of dollars for it, crated it out to the Arizona desert, and rebuilt it brick by brick. Then feeling a bridge doesn't look quite right without water flowing under it, they created an artificial lake for it to stand over.

Can you wonder that I love the madness that is America?

To top it all, Robert McCulloch, the oil magnate who bought the bridge, was bitterly disappointed. He hadn't been to see the bridge he was buying and thought he was getting Tower Bridge, the one with the Gothic towers and wrought ironwork that opens in the middle. Instead, he'd shipped to Arizona quite an ordinary-looking old stone bridge.

To film *The Special London Bridge Special*, they even imported a real English double-decker bus to drive across the bridge, with me as a London clippie yelling, "Fares please."

I must say it was a very strange feeling to see the bridge standing in the middle of nowhere surrounded by palm trees and sunshine. As a child, I had sung:

London Bridge is falling down,
dance o'er my lady lea.

Then I crossed it under such different circumstances and it was quite eerie to cross it in Havasu, USA. Strangely enough, I never saw the beauty of London Bridge until I saw it in Arizona. Now I'm delighted that the bridge is alive and well and living at Lake Havasu.

In *The Special London Bridge Special*, Tom Jones hopped on my bus and asked for a ticket for the whole journey. I delivered his ticket along with the line, "I'm so glad you're going all the way!"

The delight of that show for me was singing a duet with Tom Jones. *What's New Pussycat?* was one of my favourite films and I loved the way he sang its theme song. For weeks I'd gone round trying to hum that song, but it's not a hummable song. Tom tried teaching me the words, but I never managed to give the "whoa wo" quite the same sex appeal he gave it.

The duet Tom and I sang together in the special was written by Ronnie Cass, who'd written some of my best revue material with darling Peter Myers. This time Ronnie wrote us a nostalgic number called "I Miss London Town". A great song, and how divine it was to gaze into Tom's eyes as I sang it.

I hadn't seen Ronnie or Peter for several years until one night I was doing a cabaret act at the Bagatelle Club and I spotted them in the audience. The last faces I wanted to see were theirs because I happened to be singing one of their numbers at the time. From whence comes the expression "caught in the act".

I smiled at them sweetly, finished my act, and tried to run out of the stage door as quickly as I could, but they cornered me, and before I could say, "The royalty cheque's in the post," they launched into a speech about my song being their song. Some writers (including me!) are so terribly possessive about their material. I've always been very good about giving my writers credit, but it's usually the cash they're after.

However, on that occasion, Peter and Ronnie paid me—with the lovely compliment of saying, "If it was anyone else, we'd sue, but no one ever performs our material as well as you."

The film *Jules Verne's Rocket to the Moon* was shot in Dublin, for some inexplicable reason. I played the headmistress of a school for wayward girls, and I only agreed to go to Ireland because of the prawns. I had visions of unlimited Dublin Bay prawns for every meal. But, as luck would have it, it seems the only place in the world you can't get Dublin Bay prawns is in Dublin.

When I was asked to make a movie in New York for once, I was delighted. *Harvey Middleman—Fireman* was a mad film written and directed by Ernest Pintoff in which Gene Troobnick was a man who still wanted a bedtime story read to him, and I was the crazy marriage guidance counsellor who read it.

I was keen to get back to live theatre again and went to Princeton, New Jersey to play in *Charley's Aunt*. I played his aunt who comes from Brazil—where the nuts come from. I also went to Los Angeles to try out *Dumas and Son*, but the show didn't transfer to Broadway.

Meanwhile, a book I'd written came out. I called it *Sirens Should Be Seen and Not Heard*. Hirschfield drew a wonderful cartoon of me that we used for the front of the jacket. The book contained a mishmash of stories on subjects ranging from Eskimos to fallout shelters; some bizarre, some semiautobiographical, and some whimsical, but all I hope funny.

Sirens Should Be Seen and Not Heard got very good reviews. *Vogue* said of my book: "The book is hand-printed in black on a white background. The matching jacket is particularly pleasing. It is in sheer paper and though it looks casual, it is elegant enough for the early evening."

I interspersed each story with Aunt Hermione's agony column, where I answered made-up, mad questions such as:

Dear Hermione,
    My fox fur sneaks out at night and comes back with its jaws full of feathers. What do you advise?

My advice was: "Either chain up your fur or move to the city."

Dear Hermione,

My trusty old mother has been sold a plot of land on the moon for two-thousand dollars. She has received a prettily coloured certificate from the Moonbeam Development Corporation but there is no possession date given and I see that their lawyers are Wynken, Blynken, and Nod. Do you know this firm?

—Suspicious

Dear Suspicious,

Yes, I have known this firm for years. They are completely trustworthy.

—Aunt Hermione

I'd used a similar format in my earlier book, *The World Is Square*, and I've seen the idea copied by others many times since. One of my letters came from "Lady Killer, Central Park" and asked how to remove bloodstains from white-kid gloves. I advised an ex-millionairess: "No matter how old your diamonds are do not throw them away. You will find they can still be used for many useful purposes such as scratching your initials on glass. Or why not dye your diamonds brilliant red and wear them as rubies."

My favourite letters and replies were from two fiancés; one wrote:

Dear Aunt Hermione,

My fiancée asked me to supper last week and served what seemed to be curried lamb. But when I complained later in the evening about violent indigestion, she told me she had curried an old wool jumper.

To which I replied:

It was Madame Du Barry, I think, who made the now-famous remark, "Anything that is edible can be curried."

185

Though currying an old wool jumper is going too far. It may, of course, have been intended for a joke. If so, it was in rather bad taste.

And my advice to his unfortunate fiancée was:

Even if your fiancé told you to go and boil your head, it was silly of you to do so. Your life together cannot fail to be unharmonious if you allow him to boss you about like this, and the fact that boiling has improved your appearance does nothing to alter my opinion.

I enjoyed going round publicising the book, especially when I began to be invited to lecture at ladies' luncheon clubs and to delegations of nuclear physicists. I particularly loved going to an organisation called Daughters of the British Empire; they treated me as if I *were* the British Empire.

I remember that at one luncheon in America I was ushered on to the dais and I sat down: as I did so, a lady in a hat rushed up to me and in a rather pompous way yelled, "You can't sit there —that's the President's chair." I loathe ungraciousness and pomposity, and when she added, "and I am the President," I couldn't resist saying quite loudly, "Oh, I thought Mr Nixon was the President." This got a huge laugh from her oppressed electorate.

On another occasion, I heard a luncheon club organiser deliver the immortal line: "Don't sit on the dais, Doris."

For the most part, I enjoy the strange array of publicity or charity functions I'm invited to, but experience has taught me to be wary of some of the "just over the bridge and twenty minutes from town" functions. I now ask, "What town?" I also ask who will be picking me up and what in, as I'll never forget the time I agreed to speak at a hospital fund-raising charity lunch. I'd been asked to talk about myself (a favourite subject with me), and to collect me, they sent a sweet but harassed housewife driving a very old station wagon. On arrival she said, "To keep you amused, I've brought along my four children." They, in turn, had brought along their four pets. I was wearing a rather smart black wool dress on which their favourite white-angora rabbit's fur could really be shown off to its best advantage.

The one thing I now refuse to do is to judge costume balls or beauty competitions, because judging these can make you an entirely new set of enemies, which I need like a hole in the head. The ones I have now are just as good as the day I first made them.

My concert career continued to flourish and I went round reciting *Peter and the Wolf*, *The Carnival of the Animals*, and Poulenc's *Babar, the Elephant* with various American symphony orchestras, as well as repeating *Façade*, and recording it for Decca.

I was also asked to make a record of Aristophanes' play *Lysistrata*, which was enormous fun to do. They assembled an excellent cast that included Stanley Holloway. I loved playing Lysistrata, although in playing an ancient Greek matriarch of power and determination who used sex as a weapon I was clearly cast against type.

Another recording offer came from the Vienna Philharmonic Orchestra. They asked me to make a record with them narrating *Peter and the Wolf* and *The Carnival of the Animals* with Karl Bohm conducting. I was in London at the time and recorded it there wearing earphones, while the orchestra recorded in Vienna. It's not at all easy making a record with an orchestra that isn't even in the same country. It took us all day and I'm only surprised it didn't take us all week. When I was awarded a Grammy for it, no one was more surprised than I.

The producers, Polydor and Deutsche Grammophon, were very good to work for and asked me whether I would like them to fill my room at the recording studios with champagne.

I told them "Oh, no, please. I've got three years to go before I drink champagne again; I'd much prefer marzipan."

"Marzipan?" they asked incredulously.

"Yes, I adore marzipan and I'd much prefer it to champagne." They agreed readily and when I arrived at the studio, my room was filled with every sort of marzipan delight you can think of—marzipan fruits, marzipan sticks, little animals too beautiful to eat, fruitcake with marzipan topping, Battenberg rolls and petit fours. At the end of the day, I felt quite ill.

Strangely enough, at that time I was going through a rare loverless period, albeit extremely brief. It's hard to understand, even I don't understand it, but I hardly ever think of myself as single. Mind you, I hardly ever thought of myself as married when I was—and look at the trouble that got me into.

I never feel I'm being used by men. I use men as they use me. A woman is no more a sex object than a man is. I hope I've made a lot of men happy and what I did, I did with dignity. Fortunately, AIDS wasn't with us then and thank goodness, because I would have been a likely candidate to get it—quite a few of my lovers have been bisexual. Fortunately, I think I've been spared that monstrous plague. But my nights of love were not over yet—not by any means.

One morning in 1969 among the bills, begging letters, and fan mail that kick each day off to such a jolly start, I received a script that seemed more promising than many that roll in. The first-page character list revealed a cast of eleven men—and me; promising indeed. The play wasn't bad, either.

I'm known among writers as "Queen Cut"; surprisingly some also think of me as a prude, for I hate dirty jokes and smutty material. Back in revue days, if hopeful writers took Charles Hickman smutty sketches that they'd written for me, Charles would tell them firmly, "No, Mum wouldn't like that—it's rude." Also, I do not like nudity, although in the right place nudity—if properly handled—can be marvellous.

After many cuts and rewrites, and a particularly fearsome row when I refused to say the word *lavatory* onstage, I agreed to do Robert Tanich's play in the West End. It was called *Highly Confidential* and judging from the number of people who came to see it, highly confidential is what it remained. A nice man called Malcolm Farquar was the director, but we found him something to do.

The play was a wonderful vehicle for me as Agnes Derringdo, a spy who was once voted spy of the year for trying to blow up the Bosphorus. She was a combination of Mata Hari and James Bond. Robert wrote some funny lines, such as "Pack a magnum of champagne and one slipper"; "There's roast flamingo for lunch —tell cook to stuff it"; and on hearing I was to be shot at dawn I drawled, "At dawn? I'll never be ready." I suppose there weren't enough funny lines, for the play was slaughtered by the critics and only ran three months. You see, I tell the bad as well as the good in this tell-all. That was the bad, though in fairness to myself my personal reviews were ecstatic; my favourite was by Peter Lewis, who said, "She is with us again like a rare orchid that blooms extravagantly every seven years."

The opening night at the Cambridge Theatre was the most disastrous I have ever lived through.

One actor was supposed to come on reading an important "plot point" out of a newspaper. I didn't know, but apparently he hadn't bothered to learn his speech and he wandered on searching every page of the newspaper trying to find where he'd written his words. Fortunately I knew them, grabbed the newspaper, and said them for him. Another actor completely missed his entrance and left me on the stage reciting "Jabberwocky" to fill in. Two other actors "clinked glasses" over-enthusiastically, showering the stage with glass and blood and spoiling a "poisoned drink" gag that I was supposed to perform next with the same glasses. To top it all, a stagehand accidentally lowered the safety curtain in the middle of the first act.

Despite the play, it was fun to be back in London. Anne Clements popped into my life again, this time from behind a tree in dear old Kinnerton Street, where I'd rented a mews cottage. She was a full-time drama student now and became a pal— though she did get me into some scrapes. Because of her, I got inveigled into performing at a tango tea at the end of Brighton Pier. If you learn anything at all from this book, let it be that if you're invited to a tango tea at the end of Brighton Pier—say *no*.

Anney was staying with me the night the first man landed on the moon. She persuaded me to stay up till dawn to watch it live on TV and I'm so glad I did. Of course, I was a little disappointed that they didn't find any funny little men with pop eyes and turnip hands there, but it was still incredible to think men were actually standing on the moon. When I was born, the aeroplane hadn't even been invented and my mother told me the moon was made of blue cheese. Now we can reach the moon, but you still can't get a plumber on a Sunday.

In London I resumed my affair with Beaudoin, who had now become a successful antique dealer. Feeling it was time we formalised our relationship, we got engaged. Unfortunately our engagement was discovered by the press, who insisted upon revealing my age as seventy-four and stated his age as being thirty-three. My comment, "He loves antiques—I think that's why he fell for me," became quote of the week in the London papers.

Many older men marry young girls and no one thinks anything of it. Things are slightly better now, but then I felt I was striking a blow for women's lib. Not that I consider myself a feminist, and last time I travelled on the *Q. E. II*, I was aware it would no longer be a case of women and children first. I rather like Bernard Shaw's

190

words, "Why try to be equal when women used to be men's superiors?"

Of course, Beaudoin and I never did get married. At the time, I was better off than he was and I've never felt I could marry someone poorer than I. Of course, now he's a lot wealthier than I am and, when I come to think about it, he's still unmarried and so am I—and we never did break off our engagement.

At one shocking moment of time, I realised I was simultaneously engaged to Beaudoin and Peter Bull, but the truth was none of us intended to marry.

I'll end this London idyll with my favourite line from *Highly Confidential*: "As one grows older, culture takes the place of sex—*no?*" "No" was my very definite answer.

I left Beaudoin behind in London and returned to my flat in New York.

Noël Coward still had his pied-à-terre in the same building, so I saw him whenever he was in New York. He seemed to be getting very frail. In 1970 I was about to tour South Africa with *Fallen Angels* and *Fumed Oak*. I was directing the productions myself and I found one or two holes and weak spots in *Fumed Oak*. I asked Noël whether he knew and he said, "Yes dear, I wrote it very quickly." Tentatively I said, "Would you mind if I fixed it up a bit?" and he said, "Not at all." I knew then he must be ill.

The last time I saw him was at his seventieth birthday party. He looked at me and said, "How awfully sad it is to be seventy." I said, "It's not sad—when you think of the alternative," which cheered him up no more than it deserved to. It *was* sad, though. It always is to see very beautiful people getting old. If it's someone who's just been attractive, you don't mind so much.

My last contact with Noël was when he sent me a telegram for the first night of *A Little Night Music*. It just said: "Darling Boodles, Great success and much love, Noël." I thought it was very sweet of him to bother. After all, I had never sent him a telegram.

My journey to South Africa to do *Fallen Angels* was arduous to say the least, as I still refused to fly. I sailed to Cape Town on an Italian ship as filthy as a sink, and the journey was so rough that I had to be lashed to the mast. I then caught a train called the Transkaroo Express and I arrived in Johannesburg exhausted and upset, for I'd already seen several official signs saying, NO BLACKS ALLOWED HERE. One was outside a station waiting room and one was above a phone box saying, WHITES ONLY TO USE THIS TELEPHONE. I was appalled.

Joan Heal was playing Julia in *Fallen Angels* and we didn't get on; she tried too hard to be funny onstage, which, of course, is the kiss of death to any production. My dressing room at the Alexander Theatre was so dirty that I insisted on it being washed out. It wasn't being done properly, so I did it myself and was a little surprised when Joan asked me whether I'd wash hers out, too.

There was a pervasive feeling of hate in the air in Johannesburg, and I don't just mean in the theatre.

I was keen to see the real South Africa, so when some nuns invited me to visit a Roman Catholic convent school in Soweto, I was delighted. I was appalled at the conditions in the black township; there were no streets or pavements, just a muddy waste of shanties crowded much too close together. The nuns led me to a hut that was used as the school.

The children had been warned of my visit and in unison they said "good day" very politely and we had tea, then I was called upon to recite. The natural language of the children was Sotho and I am sure they did not understand half of what I was saying, but they laughed in all the right places and when I lowered my voice to represent a man, the laughter was so loud I had to repeat it.

I was told the schools were far too few and oversubscribed. The children looked upon school as a ticket to higher things and no one missed a day except through severe illness, as there was always someone waiting to take their places.

The nuns drove me back to the hotel, talking and gesticulating

192

all the way. "God will take care of us all" seemed to be their philosophy. I didn't like to tell them I didn't believe in God.

Back in the hotel, a Japanese business team had arrived and were made temporary whites so they could stay there. I hated Johannesburg and all it stood for.

On the way home, I managed to squeeze in a family visit to England. Whether it was because I'd come from South Africa or not I don't know, but the immigration officer seemed reluctant to let me into the country.

"Why do you want to enter Britain?" he queried.

"I've come to see my two children—both of whom are older than I am."

He obviously didn't have a sense of humour, for he looked very stern and said, "How strange. Now Miss Gingold, I'm sorry to tell you but I'm afraid there's a severe irregularity on your embarkation card. Here by your passport number, you're supposed to enter your date of birth."

"What have I put?" I asked.

"You've put—'guess!'"

Now the world is so overcrowded with terrorists I suppose we must expect stern immigration officials. I love question seven on the US Immigration form: "Do you intend to take up arms or offer violence against the Constitution of the USA?" It is so tempting to write: "Sole purpose of visit."

I sorted out my little local difficulty with the British immigration officer; he let me into the country and I went up to Scotland to see my son Leslie. He was married by now with two boys of his own.

I had never met David and Robert before. They seemed nice little boys with broad Scots accents. They were running along saying, "Auch, it's me Granny—it's me Granny."

I looked around to see where their granny was—then the horrendous realisation dawned that it was me! I was their granny!

They tell me that I hit them with my umbrella and told them never to use that obscene word again. I can't believe I did, but *Granny* isn't a word of which I am fond. I'm happy to say Leslie's boys have now grown into charming young men.

One never knows who or what is round the next corner. Fate is so inscrutable. If only she would occasionally drop a hint, it would help.

In 1975 the phone rang and a nice young man called Kurt Adler from the San Francisco Opera Company, which, I'd been told, is the only opera company that makes any money, said, "How would you like to sing in opera?"

Naturally, I told him he had the wrong number and gave him Placido Domingo's, but no, he said, they were doing Donizetti's *La Fille du Régiment* and would rather have me as he thought I would make a better Duchess of Krakenthorp than Domingo.

Of course, I wasn't expected to sing and they really only wanted me to play Beverley Sills's mother and say, "Hello this is my daughter." It didn't seem worth going to San Francisco to say one line, so I turned it down. The nice young man was very persuasive and kept ringing and offering me greater financial inducements and artistic carrots, such as wanting me to write my own scene and allowing me to sing.

I was shocked at first. "Won't Donizetti be offended?" The young man promised he wouldn't tell Donizetti and assured me that, as the opera was a light one, it would be quite acceptable to add some dialogue.

Finally, I agreed to do it provided they sent a knight in shining armour on a horse to meet me at the San Francisco railway station. I felt sure this would put Mr Adler off, but he didn't even pause for breath.

"Of course, we wouldn't dream of letting you enter town without one!"

I'd almost forgotten my stipulation until my train pulled into the station and there was my knight sitting on a horse blowing a trumpet. He presented me with a huge bouquet of roses. Quite a crowd gathered—a film crew and press photographers (the young man was no fool!). I made a gracious speech that ended: "Thank you so much for this beautiful bouquet." I looked at the flowers and the horse had eaten all the heads off the roses. I have a photograph of the event in this book. You can tell which is me and which is the horse, I think.

There were many posters up around San Francisco for *La Fille du Régiment*. It advertised the guest artists to be Sills, Malas, and Gingold. There was an asterisk by my name and at the bottom of the poster, it said: MAKING HER AMERICAN OPERATIC DEBUT.

I made my entrance speaking in French—"Bon soir, Mesdames et Messieurs. Je suis enchantée de faire votre connaissance et je suis ravie . . ."—until an actor stopped me in my tracks and whispered something in my ear. Surprised, I queried, "*La Fille du Régiment* in English? Well really, someone should have told me!"

I don't think Beverley Sills liked me very much because I got laughs and she didn't.

My operatic debut proved to be a big success, although I still had qualms about offending Donizetti. It seems I needn't have worried, for *Time* magazine said they couldn't tell where Donizetti stopped and Gingold started.

In fact, I was asked to repeat my performance a few years later with the New York City Opera, but unfortunately I had an accident while touring with *Side by Side with Sondheim* that prevented it.

Life is full of surprises and who knows, a whole new career could have opened up for me. *La Fille* one year, *Tosca* the next.

No one asked me to sing *Tosca*, but I soon got over my disappointment by dining at the White House. The dinner was part of the 1976 bicentennial celebrations and with President Ford and the Queen and Prince Philip present, it really was a night to remember. I bought a new dress for the occasion and I stayed at the Watergate Hotel. My former maid Sue, who had moved to Washington, came over to dress me.

The only other British actress there was Greer Garson—I suppose we represented the British theatre. Ella Fitzgerald was also there. I assumed she represented the musical world, but she laughed and said, "No, dear, I'm the token black." I looked around and sadly it did seem to have a ring of truth about it.

The White House looked simply wonderful. The flowers were magnificent and every room was full of them. There was a large tent erected in the garden in which the dinner was served while a string orchestra played. The Queen and Prince Philip stood in the entrance to the tent greeting everybody. I was pleased to notice that Greer Garson and I did wonderful curtseys, far better than anyone else's. Queen Elizabeth looked absolutely divine, really beautiful, and Prince Philip, remembering me from our London encounters, was most amusing.

All the important people sat at a long table, while we sat at round tables. The tent was very elegant—well, as elegant as a tent can be, but it was a trifle draughty. My new evening dress had a very low back and as my back was in a direct line with the draught, I surreptitiously took my linen table napkin and draped it across my back. As I was facing into the room, I felt sure no one would notice.

I was so busy enjoying myself that I failed to see that a TV camera had been set up just behind our table and there in shot—for all the viewers to see—was my table napkin. I was mortified when in the morning all my most tactful friends rang me up to say, "It was lovely to see you at the White House last night, but why did you go dressed in a table napkin?"

After a superb dinner, we went inside to the ballroom, where we had a concert and then President Ford led off the dancing; he bumped into everything but did his best.

The following night was wonderful, too. The Queen invited us to a "return match" on the royal yacht *Britannia*.

It was a very special two days for me, and I was thrilled to have been invited to both events.

I received another honour that year by being made a Dame of the Knights of Malta. England had never seen fit to give me a British Damehood—which doesn't surprise me at all. But I was delighted to become a Maltese Dame. I had to go to New York's St Patrick's Cathedral for the dubbing ceremony. It was quite painless and actually rather impressive. After the ceremony, they told me I was entitled to call myself Dame Hermione, but I never do, as I feel people may think I'm a British Dame and, as I'm not, I feel it would be rather false; but I am awfully proud of being a Dame of the Maltese Order.

Of course, one of the marvellous things about living in America is that sooner or later practically everyone gets an award of some sort. You don't have to be talented or famous either; you can get an award for being the billionth person to cross the Brooklyn Bridge or the millionth customer to pass through the doors of a department store. Or you can get a trophy for being the best-dressed mother, or for eating the most ice cream, or you can become a queen of something. These are much-prized awards and there is really no limit to the things of which you can become queens.

Since I've lived in New York, I've received the Donaldson Award, the Golden Globe (foreign press) Award, a Tony nomination, a Grammy, my award from the United Nations, the Arthur Murray Award for doing a rather dubious *paso doble* on TV, the cinema Box Office Blue Ribbon Award, the Helen Curtis Award for being the best coiffed woman on TV, the Jan Mitchell Award for "Exceptional Devotion to Dogs", the Gordons Vodka Good Gal Award for "Deeds that help to make the world a better place", and an award from the Boy Scouts of America, which rather puzzled me as I couldn't think what I had done to deserve it, except perhaps that I had left them severely alone. I've also been presented with a wall plaque from something called The Anti-Defamation League—that just *had* to be a mistake! One of my prettiest awards is the Clean Sweep Award, which I was given in 1963. It's a silver trophy with a cleaning lady holding a bucket and some brushes and mops on the top, but I never display this one, in case my visiting English chums misinterpret it and suspect I've been a housemaid over here.

Around this time, I discovered the joys of doing TV commercials, only the most tasteful ones of course, but I adored doing them—especially when I found out that you can collect an enormous fee for a day's work. Then you can just sit back and relax for the next two years while fat residual fees pour through your letter box. My favourite was when I became the Coco Goya lady and sang of the joys of coconut cream that "hits the spotta of the society snobbsa, with whom I hobnobbsa."

I think it was dear Alan Haydock of the noncommercial BBC who in an interview once asked me to do a commercial for myself. I thought he must be out of his tiny Chinese mind, but he was such a nice man, I had a go.

Miss Gingold is absolutely delightful if taken in small doses. She's an elegant addition to any salon, but do not leave her

198

about the house as she's extremely dangerous to small children. She doesn't clean up well, but although she's very expensive, she gives excellent value for money.

When I was asked to audition for Hal Prince, my immediate reaction was: "I haven't done an audition for forty years and I don't intend to restart now." When I heard it was for the new Sondheim musical *A Little Night Music*, temptation overcame pride. (It so often does.)

So I pulled out my sheet music and my tap shoes and off I went. Of course, in reality it was a most sophisticated audition and almost painless. It led to me being asked whether I would play the part of Madame Armfelt, a rich and ageing courtesan—a character part, of course.

At one stage, Hal said the part was all but mine; their only worry was that they weren't sure I could age enough to play the part of a seventy-four-year-old woman. "But Mr Prince," I told him, "I *am* seventy-four."

It was a wonderful role in a wonderful show, with lines like "I don't object to the immorality of your life—merely its sloppiness." How could I fail? I played it for nearly two years on Broadway and was nominated for a Tony for it. At first I was pleased and then they told me my nomination was for best supporting actress. That didn't please me at all—who was I supporting? It made me sound like a brassière. The final humiliation came when I didn't even win it. Still, I suppose it was better than being nominated for most-promising newcomer.

The music and lyrics of Stephen Sondheim are superb; the man is a genius. There's no song in any of his musicals that isn't part of the show—the songs all serve the show. I had a showstopping number called "Liaisons", where Madame Armfelt reminisces on her past profitable loves as being "a pleasurable means to a measurable end". She sings delicious rhyming couplets like:

I acquired some position—
plus a tiny Titian

Some directors hate actors, but Hal loves them, and he listens to them, too. He may not say yes, but he will listen. He has enormous patience and is a perfectionist. Everything has to be the best. During the Broadway run, I found I was losing weight and the prop ring I wore in the show was getting too big for me, so I substituted a tighter one. He saw the show, came round and asked, "Herman," (Hal always called me Herman) "Herman, why did you change your ring?" He doesn't miss a thing.

He was marvellous to work for, though the leading lady, Glynis Johns, and I were not overly happy with each other. I found her so unpredictable. During the final days of rehearsal, Glynis developed bronchitis, laryngitis, and a sinus infection. She was rushed to hospital with nervous exhaustion, but as soon as she heard there were plans to replace her with Tammy Grimes, she made a miraculous recovery and arrived back in time for the opening night.

I admit Glynis did bring her own fragile vulnerability to the part of Desirée, and on her good nights, it worked like magic; but I think she found it hard to reproduce night after night and her performance became erratic.

My understudy was a delicious Greek woman who hardly spoke any English, but Hal Prince was fond of her and gave her the chance to understudy me—confident I'd live up to my reputation for never being off, I suppose. But unfortunately one day when I was on my way to a matinée, I ran for a cab, fell into a pothole, and had to go to hospital to have my arm put in a sling. So my understudy had a chance to play. I believe she was quite a good actress, but not one word she spoke was understood by anyone. The management begged me to play at the evening performance, sling or not. From the audience's point of view, the sling was a stage prop and rather fitted in with my first entrance, which was in a wheelchair anyway. At least they understood what I was saying.

The last night of *A Little Night Music* on Broadway was almost as sad for me as the last night of *Sweetest and Lowest* had been in London. I always try and make every dressing room I'm in a home. Even if I'm only going to be in it for three nights, I try and put up my own curtains, set up my portable bed, and cover everything in sight with blue chintz; and I had been in my dressing room at the Majestic Theatre for nearly two years.

I shed my first tears when I found my nameplate had been taken off my dressing room door, and I shed more when I looked around the dressing room's interior and realised I'd have to get a bigger flat if I wanted to take all my belongings home. To make matters worse, enormous baskets of flowers, farewell presents from cast and fans, and piles of telegrams started arriving. Just before the half-hour was called, Hal Prince and Steve Sondheim rang from Majorca to say good-bye. It's very difficult to say a tearful good-bye on the telephone, especially when you keep thinking how much each sob is costing them.

Somehow we got through the show—the audience was ecstatic and the cast slightly hysterical. "No speeches", we'd been told by the management; so after the final curtain, Glynis and the rest of the cast went back to their dressing rooms—not a dry eye among them.

The audience showed no signs of leaving and they started clapping in rhythm. I stood around in the wings because it sounded to me like an audience that wouldn't leave until it was asked.

"All right," said the stage manager, "get them out but keep it short." So I went out in front of the curtain and said, "I'm a prissy Englishwoman, so I never use four-letter words, but *love* is a four-letter word and that is what tonight is about. You have shown your love for us and we thank you and love you back. You are the most adorable, attractive, and appreciative darlings, but electricity is very expensive and the management humbly asks you to go home so they can turn out the lights."

The lights of *A Little Night Music* were turned out on Broadway only to be turned on in London. I went over to start rehearsals for the West End opening.

Jean Simmons replaced Glynis and all was well. I like Jean enormously. She's sweet, she's charming, she's talented, she's beautiful—I should hate her. Jean had professional discipline and was great fun, too. She taught me to play backgammon; we kept the board set up in my dressing room and played in the intervals between shows on matinée days.

I'm so glad I had the chance to make my farewell West End appearance in a smash hit. As in New York, Madame Armfelt made most of her appearances either being pushed in a wheelchair or hobbling on a stick. I loved the idea of all my London chums watching the show and thinking, "Poor old thing can't even walk now." Then I surprised them by rushing forward in full fettle to take the curtain call.

When they asked me whether I would like to do the film of *A Little Night Music*, I was delighted. Elizabeth Taylor was to play Desirée. Elizabeth is one of my very favourite ladies. I was surprised to find she has an outrageously wicked sense of humour, and I loved doing the film with her. She is extremely generous. When we finished filming, she gave me a beautiful gold lorgnette as a memento of our association. Of course, Elizabeth had to sing in the film, and did so very successfully. She worked hard on her voice and studied her musical numbers intently because she was determined to do them herself and determined they would be good. Practising in New York, she sang "Send in the Clowns" over and over again and then went on to record it in London, where she had a whole session with the orchestra and sang it remarkably well.

We spent four months of 1976 in Vienna shooting the film. There everyone including Elizabeth, Diana Rigg, and I put on ten pounds each. All there was to do in Vienna was eat. Everything seemed to shut down at ten o'clock, and all the people on the streets appeared to be terribly old, but the kaffee and küchen were marvellous. At that time, Elizabeth was being courted by Ardeshir Zahedi, the Iranian Ambassador to Washington. Every morning he flew a huge can of Beluga caviar to Elizabeth with his compliments. When Elizabeth found out that I loved caviar as much as she did, she invited me to share it with her. Seventy-five dollars an ounce and every morning we ate it together for breakfast, spooning it out like cereal. She couldn't have been sweeter. We also had some fun at Take Five, Vienna's top disco —what am I saying?—Vienna's only disco.

After the shooting of some early scenes, a colleague of mine who'd seen some of the rushes told me how young and well I looked. I was furious, as that was the last thing Madame Armfelt was supposed to be, and I immediately asked the makeup department whether they could age me more.

The Austrian government was anxious to make Austria popular as a film centre again, so they helped to finance the film and offered to lend us all the authentic furnishings we wanted from their museums. Consequently, in the dining room scene, we had real gold plates and I "slept" in a bed that had been slept in by Maria Theresa; all the jewellery I wore was genuine and the furniture was out of this world. We filmed in a real castle which was exquisite, except that although the Russians had left all the castle's tapestries and art treasures intact, they had taken all the plumbing. Scenically the film was superb, but in other ways it stank.

I was disappointed with the filming of my "Liaisons" number. Instead of a straight filming of me singing the song, someone had the bright idea of cutting away to shots of old Valentine cards; very pretty they were, too—I'd be the first to admit they were a lot prettier than my face—but they made the number over-nostalgically cute and it lost all its bite and cynicism. It was cut completely from the final print.

If Hal Prince had been left to direct the film on his own, he would have come up with a much better result, but "too many cooks spoil the broth"—and unfortunately that's how it got served up.

We'd only been shooting a few days when a friend told me he thought *Night Music* was going to be as big for me as *Gigi* had been. Even in these early days, some instinct told me he was wrong. Sadly, the film never even got a general release, although most of the few critics that did see it said they rather liked it. My personal favourite review was Rex Reed's in the *Daily News*, which said, "Hermione Gingold has magic to do and does it with the regal aplomb of a dowager empress stoned on Ovaltine."

I enjoyed myself enormously after the filming was over; Elizabeth kept in touch with me and we did our best to promote the film. However, during this time, my poor darling Yorkie Messy Missey died. She was fifteen years old. When I returned home to America, I found another dog waiting for me—a present from Elizabeth. I then went out on the American tour of *A Little Night Music*, with Jean Simmons playing Desirée again. All in all, that show filled four happy years of my life.

In New York I renewed my liaison with Sondheim by joining Larry Kert, Barbara Heuman, and Georgia Brown in *Side by Side with Sondheim* at the Music Box Theatre. I took over from Ned Sherrin as narrator, adding two songs: "Liaisons" and "I never do Anything Twice", a daringly suggestive Sondheim song from *The Seven Percent Solution*. I adored the song and so did the audience, but I turned down Merv Griffin's request to sing it on his show because I considered it unsuitable for TV.

Of course, I rewrote the script of *Side by Side* to suit my own personality and added some stories with a Sondheim connection, the most tenuous of which was a true story concerning my wig. My own hair has never pleased me much; I used to get a man in to mow it from time to time, and then I'd stick my head out of the window and whichever way the wind was blowing determined my style. Eventually, I did find a hairdresser who was prepared to take me on as long as I kept his name quiet. During the filming of *A Little Night Music*, I wore a heavy white wig for so long that my own hair became extra tatty, and I took to wearing another wig in private life. I was walking along the beach at Fire Island when a gust of wind blew off my wig and it landed in the sea. I walked on as if nothing had happened, but two gallant young men who were passing leapt into the sea and brought back my dripping wig, announcing in heartfelt tones, "Oh, Miss Gingold, we're sorry but we're afraid your little dog is drowned."

It was kind of them and they looked completely crestfallen when I said, "Thank you, but I have twenty more at home." Then I threw it back in the water.

When the Broadway run ended, Millicent Martin and Nancy Dussult took over from Barbara and Georgia and we took *Side by Side* to California to play it at the Huntington Hartford Theatre. I stayed there with my dear friend Russell Orton in his new home, a magnificent Beverly Hills house halfway up a canyon, with the most enormous swimming pool and a divine garden. For the benefit of English friends who wish to know what grows in American gardens, let me say that if I want an orange or lemon or an avocado, I can just stretch out my arm and pick them off the trees. It makes me very lazy to be waited on by nature. There are flowers too, of course, wonderful blooms of every colour and size. I can fill my bedroom with them and by the next day more have grown in their place. Warmed by the sun, I dress in shorts and a large red hankie that hopefully conceals the fact that I am a woman.

For a limited time, before utopia drifts to boredom, Hollywood days are bliss. Of course, the nights should be bliss too, but at that time they were marred for me by my drive home up the canyon after the theatre.

I usually drive with both hands over my ears, which makes me a very dangerous driver. To make matters worse, I don't know my left hand from my right unless I'm wearing a wedding ring. Fortunately, I go so slowly that I've never hit anyone yet. Russell's canyon seemed to be full of coyotes, owls, snakes, muggers, and all sorts of other wildlife that come out at night.

I got sick and sometimes very frightened at night driving up the twisty canyon, so I decided to ask round the theatre and find out whether there was someone who'd drive me to and from the show. One of the understudies said, "I've got just the person for you. He's a good actor but hasn't worked for a year and is about to kill himself. He doesn't need the money; he's inherited a fortune and just wants something to do."

I said, "Splendid. Ask him to come and see me and we'll discuss proper terms."

We settled on terms agreeable to both of us. He was tall, dark, young, wealthy, and very handsome. In fact, he seemed—quite satisfactory. That is how Little Big Boy came into my life. Little Big Boy is an Indian name of which I'm rather fond. I'm using it because Little Big Boy says his mother would not like his name to be mentioned, and I promised him it wouldn't be.

Although to start with Little Big Boy was simply my driver, we found we had a lot in common and the more we talked, the more we liked one another. I found him very attractive and I could tell he was not disinterested in me.

206

Russell was going to the South of France on holiday, and before he left he asked, "Would you like me to get someone to stay in the house while I'm gone? . . . Just to look after the sordid things that you never think of, such as closing windows and doors?"

"So you don't trust me," I said, "well if I need any help, I can ask Little Big Boy to come over."

Russell paused.

"Ah," I continued, "so it's as I suspected—you don't like him."

"It's not that I don't like him," replied Russell. "I just think he's too young for you."

"I don't think age makes any difference. Both my husbands were the same age as I was and they were both flops."

Russell had no answer to that.

The next night, I took Little Big Boy to a cast party and told him about Russell's leaving and asked, "Do you want to come up the hill and live with me?" He said he did. We kissed, and left the party—it was quite a good one too, the party that is, but we left early and went home.

I know he thought he was in love with me, and I knew I loved him. We went to bed together as friends and made love while the nightingales sang us to sleep. In the morning, we woke up to the sound of mocking birds whistling in the sunlight. My dog, who usually slept on the bed with me, had been replaced now.

Little Big Boy was still asleep, so I went downstairs and made breakfast, took it upstairs to our room, and Little Big Boy got up. We ate, made love, put on our swimsuits, and went down to the pool, where we played games in the water.

When *Side by Side* ended, I went back to New York to film *Garbo Talks*, which Sidney Lumet directed. It starred Anne Bancroft and Dorothy Loudon, and I had a small cameo part.

Little Big Boy sold his flat in California and joined me in New York. He moved into my flat and we lived together for five happy years, which was longer than I lived with either of my husbands.

In many ways, we were perfectly suited. The only trouble was that he was twenty-six and I was eighty-one. In spite of our age difference, we enjoyed the same things and made each other laugh. We had a marvellous sex life, too. Although I must confess that after I turned eighty-five, I found sex wasn't as important to me as it had been when I was eighty. This confession surprises even me, because up till then, I had always been a sex maniac.

Gradually, Little Big Boy found two things. First, my flat was big enough for one but not for two people. Secondly, I was very jealous and he was not. Also, the press began to get interested in our relationship and started to try and make something of our age difference. One gossip snippet said: "Who is the dishy young man so often seen escorting Hermione Gingold about town? He looks like a cross between John Travolta and the Marlboro man. Watch this space."

Little Big Boy had his pride, and talk about us began to upset him.

When he left, I found the bottom had fallen out of my world. A little boy had turned into a big man and wanted no more of me. I realised that it had to happen sooner or later, but that didn't make it any easier to bear. All the rules say I'm too old to love, but it still hurts me and I find it painful to write about. So I won't.

After *Garbo Talks*, I decided to take a holiday—in London, of course. I was told a good many artists give talks on the *Queen Elizabeth II* in return for a free passage for themselves and a friend. I couldn't believe it was true, but it was. I liked the arrangement and next thing I knew, I was on board—without an idea in my head what my talk was to be about.

The other speaker aboard ship was Carroll O'Connor, and I felt sure he would get the bigger welcome, though actually we both got full houses. The manager of talks asked me what mine was to be called. I said I didn't know as I hadn't decided yet, but it would be completely ad lib.

"You must give it a name," he said, "so I can announce it in the ship's newspaper."

I thought for a minute. Nothing came to mind but "How to grow old—disgracefully!" I thought that, at least, would shut him up.

"Fabulous!" he said, and that is how this book came by its name.

The talk was indeed nothing but ad lib, and fortunately not only very funny but also a great success. After the talk, I invited questions from the audience and one man asked, "Miss Gingold, do you think there is sex after death?"

"Oh," I said, "I do hope so."

In London I stayed at Anne's lovely house in Westminster and fell in love with little Hermione, my god-daughter—as children go, this one's not bad.

Anne's husband, Reggie, was Under Secretary of State for Trade at the time and they arranged all sorts of outings for me—lunch at Lloyds, a Guildhall visit, and a party with the American ambassador at Winfield House. They also organised a lunch in my honour at the House of Commons with Paul Channon, the then Arts Minister. I was allowed to invite my sister and all my dearest English chums—well, those still alive, that is. Charles Hickman (the director from *Sweet and Low*), Donald Neville Willing (Café de Paris), Beaudoin, Russell Harty, and David Jacobs.

Prince Charles was just about to marry Lady Diana Spencer and England was gripped with royal wedding fervour. Anney's father managed to get us front-row seats in a building right opposite the entrance to St Paul's Cathedral to watch the wedding procession!

It was a wonderful day and by chance all the world's media were assembled in the same building as we were. Barbara Walters spotted me and gave me her press badge. We watched as the honoured guests left their limousines to walk up the steps into the cathedral, and then an enormous cheer spread through the crowd and we thought the Queen must be arriving—or at the very least the Queen Mother. The recipient of the cheer was none other than the corporation dustcart gritting the road. That typical example of the British sense of humour made me feel very proud to be English.

Then we saw Nancy Reagan arriving; she looked so elegant that I found myself very proud of her too; and I realised I truly belonged to both continents.

Little Big Boy flew over to escort me back to America on the boat. I used the same title again for my talk, but with different material. During the questions, one lady called out, "Do you think a picture hat enhances the face?" I replied, "At my age, no, I need a frame."

After my affair with Little Big Boy ended, I knew the best therapy for me was, as always, to throw myself into my work. Perhaps I overdid this, as I chose to tour America with *Side by Side*, covering 30,000 miles and 60 cities.

I enjoyed the tour but I found it very tiring; it was what is known as a "bus and truck" tour. This means the show's scenery, costumes, and props travel in a truck, while the artists and orchestra go in a bus. Sometimes we'd spend ten hours travelling in the coach and do a show the same evening. Often we'd play the same city for a week or two, but other places we might only do one performance. Some very strange venues we played, too. In the Deep South, we found the theatre was what they call "a cow palace", an enormous hall where they hold political meetings. I looked with foreboding at the stage they'd rigged up at one end, but it turned out to be one of the most exciting nights of the tour. We filled the "cow palace" with over five thousand people. Some had never seen a live stage show in their lives, but they loved it and we did seven encores.

In Memphis, Tennessee, we went to a theatre that hadn't been used for twelve years. It was fairly clean but there were no doorknobs on any of the dressing room doors. I put my foot down and said I wouldn't play the show until I had a knob on my door.

"Suppose I got trapped and couldn't get out?" I asked. A knob was soon placed on my door. After the show, the theatre manager made a big fuss of us all and insisted on serving us some rather indifferent champagne. I refused his hospitality, as I had another year to go, and then told him very firmly that his money would have been far better spent on doorknobs than on champagne.

I was pretty tired towards the end of the tour, but fortunately I'm very tough and in fact, I was the only one of the cast never to be off. That is—until we reached Kansas City. Luckily, we only had one week of the tour left, for Kansas City was my downfall, and down I went very heavily. We broke our bus and truck routine by travelling a long haul by train, arriving at the Kansas City railway station at 2:30 AM. The station was dimly lit and I couldn't find a porter. I spotted my suitcase among the luggage and went to get it. Unfortunately, an iron truck had been left in quite the wrong place; it had a long pole sticking out of it, and over the pole I went.

I shattered my knee and dislocated my right arm very badly; even as I write this, my arm still hasn't properly recovered. I was rushed to a hospital run by nuns, where I was prayed over a lot—which did me a lot of good, I'm sure. Later I went back by stretcher to New York.

211

Now here I am in my flat with round-the-clock nurses. My lovers have vanished, and all my relatives live in England. Sometimes I wonder whether I've given up too much for the theatre, but I have one big consolation—*money*. I've saved hard and invested wisely and it's amazing what a comfort filthy lucre is. Just as well, for now I'm not able to work and probably never will be again.

But I have got one great final performance left to give—my death, which is probably imminent and I hope won't be too prolonged. I'm not looking forward to it, but sometimes I can't help thinking that I might be better off playing my harp in the other place. Although I must admit that I've been such a thoroughly bad lot, I've probably got something hotter in store.

Meanwhile, I'm quite busy planning my funeral. I don't think a formal thanksgiving service where a clergyman or rabbi gets up and says what a wonderful person I've been would be quite suitable. He might say what a lot of good I'd done in my life and everyone would jeer, knowing I've never done a damn thing for anyone. No, I plan to record my own eulogy. I won't say anything too heavy, just a few words thanking people for coming. I'd better have two versions, one saying: "I didn't expect to see so many people," and in the other, "I was hoping more people would turn up." I'll let the master of ceremonies use his discretion as to which tape he plays, and then I think I'll say: "This is the last time I'll be talking to you; I do hope you all have a jolly funeral and champagne will shortly be served. It's up to you now to keep my memory alive and warn future generations not to turn out like Hermione Gingold." Then I might tell a few funny stories or even sing a number or two.

I think it's a great idea and might even start a trend. Stupidly, I told a friend and he thought it was so good, he's going to do it himself.

Of course, it's a race against time now because I want to get mine in first. But . . . I don't want to have to—if you know what I mean.

Epilogue

S adly, a few months after she wrote the last page of her book, Hermione was dead. She contracted pneumonia and this was complicated by heart disease. She was admitted to Lenox Hill Hospital in New York City, where she died three weeks later on May 24th, 1987. She was eighty-nine years old.

Fortunately, her ending was, as she'd hoped, fairly swift and painless. Her faithful housekeeper, Mary, and her nurse were by her side.

At her own request, she was cremated in New York and her ashes were taken to Los Angeles to rest in the Columbarium of the Holy Spirit, in Forest Lawn Memorial Park, Glendale, California.

Regrettably, Hermione never got around to recording her own eulogy. At her memorial service at the Church of the Recessional, no one jeered when people spoke of the good she had done, for she brought laughter to the world and it is a sadder, duller place without her.

Anne Clements Eyre
London, January 1989

Index

216

illnesses and injuries, 138–9,
   172–3, 194, 211
dies, 213
on her age, 19, 161, 190–91, 194,
   199, 208, 210
on America, 148, 166
on American troops, 85–9, 93–7,
   101–3, 119
on apartheid, 192–3
on audiences, 95
her awards, 146–7, 187, 197–8
in the Blitz, 73–4, 76, 78–9,
   89–90, 97–8, 100
on burglars, 112, 175
in cabaret, 128, 132–3
on censorship, 55–7, 76, 134
her clothes, 68, 104, 114–15, 121,
   132, 147, 148, 151
on her death, 212
as an embroiderer, 158
on Englishmen, 162
on filming, 107
on flying, 128–30
as a homemaker, 24, 59, 66, 131,
   156, 165
on interviewers, 92, 140–41,
   159–61
on intimate revue, 167
on London, 103–4, 109, 181–2
her looks, 11, 45, 80, 205
on men, 26, 170, 188
her money, 40, 42, 50, 69, 124,
   131–2, 142, 182, 212
on her name, 22–3, 95, 147
on New York, 69
on her personalities, 130–31
her pets, 41, 50, 63, 77, 79, 107,
   147, 156, 168–9, 204
on public speaking, 186–7
on sex, 35, 38–9, 45, 46, 187, 208,
   209
as a singer, 42, 53, 62, 66, 70, 81,
   123, 150, 152–3, 159, 183, 194
on the Sixties, 181–2
her taste in food, 63, 90, 119,
   187–8, 203

on women, 52
as a writer, 67, 75, 85, 88, 112,
   205
Gingold, James (father), 19, 22–5,
   28, 37–8, 44, 47, 60
Gingold, Kate (mother), 20–23, 26,
   31–2, 35, 37, 39, 44, 63, 72
Gingold, Margaret (sister), 21, 22,
   31, 37, 181, 209
Girl from UNCLE, The (TV series), 156
Godfrey, Peter, 61
"Golden Thimble Club", 158
Golding, William, 78
Goldman, Milton, 139
Goodnight Vienna (musical), 50
Gould, Elliott, 182
Graham, Ronnie, 128
"Grande Gingold" (BBC special),
   133–4
Granger, Stewart, 61
Griffin, Merv, 141, 154, 205
Grisewood, Harmon, 53
Guardian, The, 180
Guilaroff, Sydney, 151
Guthrie, Tyrone, 57

Hallmark Hall of Fame (TV show),
   156
Hamilton, Lance, 120, 122
Hannen, Nicholas, 57
Hannen, Peter, 57–8, 63
Harding, Gilbert, 134
Harris, Radie, 161
Harrison, Lillian, 53
Harty, Russell, 209
Harvey Middleman—Fireman (film),
   184
Havoc, June, 158
Hawtrey, Charles, 32–3
Hayes, Helen, 147–8
Hearne, Richard, 106
Helpmann, Robert, 61, 75
Herman, Jerry, 167
Heston, Charlton, 182
Heuman, Barbara, 205
Hewett, Chris, 96–7, 109

217